Her Husband is Known in the Gates

Her Husband is Known in the Gates

Helping Your Husband Succeed

Bernadine Bigner Cantrell

Sower's Press

Marietta, Georgia

HER HUSBAND IS KNOWN IN THE GATES: HELPING YOUR HUSBAND SUCCEED
Sower's Press, P.O. Box 666306, Marietta 30066
00 99   5

Library of Congress Catalog Card No: 95–70737

ISBN 0–9647028–3–5

Designer: Jamey Wood

To my husband, Wes

Do you see a man diligent and skillful in his business? He will stand before kings; he will not stand before obscure men.

—Proverbs 22:29

Table of Contents

Foreword

"Bernie's Book," as I call it, is the story of a woman's struggle with success, an ambitious, insensitive husband, and her deep commitment to Jesus Christ. It is an excellent work born of that struggle, and demonstrates Biblical principles applied to a situation every woman faces in one way or another. It's a real life story of Christian living.

Every woman wants her husband to prosper. Every woman wants a flourishing family. Every woman contends with control and submission. Every woman would like to talk to someone who has worked through these issues.

Through thirty-eight years of marriage, four children, sixteen grandchildren, and a husband's career, Bernie has learned many lessons that she'll share with you. Has it worked? I'd say yes! Life is not perfect, and we have disagreements; but through it all we know for sure He provides the answers.

The Lord has allowed me to be promoted from office machine repairman to president/CEO of a billion-dollar international company. I would say, however, that our greatest achievement is our family.

It is my prayer that you will find true success from God's perspective.

WESLEY E. CANTRELL
PRESIDENT/CEO
LANIER WORLDWIDE, INC.

Acknowledgments

*L*ove and appreciation to:

The man in my life, Wes, who kept saying, "You can do it."

My cherished family and cheering squad—Jamey, Kandy, Wesley, Juli, Allen, Larry, Jane, Tim, and Kristi

Bill Gothard, who taught us principles of Christian living

Mike Gilchrist, who first taught us about the abundant life

Andy Stanley, who gave me advice and encouragement

Friends across America who reviewed the principles—Carol Thigpen, Mary Jenson, Lucy Holsclaw, Claire Von Grimmenstein, Valerie Killingsworth, Dr. and Mrs. Tom Brandon, Rev. T.P. Johnston, Sandy Smith, and Allan Huber

Ladies who attended Bible classes, retreats, and Sunday School

Men who shared their thoughts about an ideal wife

Her husband is known in the city's gates, when he sits among the elders of the land.

—*Proverbs 31:23*

Wes's Story: Up the Ladder

*I*n the telling of Wes's story lies the shaping of mine.

He was an attractive, slight built young man with lots of naturally curly blond hair. He grew up with a preacher daddy in rural Georgia. The greatest thing for a young man in that community was to have a hot automobile and to appear a little rebellious. That put him **in** with the crowd. Of course, he had to run around with the guys and demonstrate by attitude and actions that he was independent and self-sufficient, which may have been even more important to the preacher's kid.

He received a good but limited public school education. He still talks about some of his teachers whose influence encouraged his good behavior and performance. Wes enjoyed his high school days with basketball and girls being his prime interests. He was smart, competitive, worked diligently to be at the head of his class, and graduated as valedictorian. As he had during his elementary years, he sought jobs to earn money. His income-making endeavors included repairing bicycles for little boys, running a newspaper route (gravel roads on a bike), and working for the local chicken farmers.

I don't know exactly what affected his next decision; it may have been finances. His dad earned minimal wages as a country preacher and principal of an elementary school. His mom was a teacher as well. There may have been other reasons, like being in a hurry or wanting to buy one of those hot automobiles. He decided to attend Southern Tech in Atlanta, Georgia, which at that time was an extension of Georgia Institute of Technology. They crammed 127 quarter-hours into his two-year education, and he graduated with honors as an electronics technician.

The attire customary for the fifties—snug fitting blue jeans, a pink shirt, white socks, white bucks, and white belt—looked great on Wes's good physique. He was dressed in this manner as he stood at the bus station on Spring Street in downtown Atlanta one afternoon, waiting for the bus to Hiram to visit his parents for the weekend.

Wes was thinking about his approaching graduation as he glanced across the street at a building whose sign read "Lanier Business Products." Only a few days earlier he had written down that name as one of the companies recruiting service technicians through the placement office at Southern Tech. He had a job promised with IBM. "Well," he thought, "it wouldn't be a bad idea to have a *temporary* job in the meantime."

Even though not appropriately dressed for a job interview, Wes made a quick decision and walked across the street. Tall, boisterous Gene Milner interviewed him and hired him immediately. Mr. Milner offered him a monthly salary of $300, but Wes persuaded him to raise it to $325.

The first time I saw Wes I thought he was one of the best looking guys I had ever met. A casual friend introduced us on my eighteenth birthday at Walgreen's drugstore on Third Street in Baton Rouge, Louisiana. What a confident young man he seemed. Totally unaware of his short stature, he had a ready smile, and an air of cockiness in his stride.

In his work, he carried a little black bag and was always dressed in a very professional manner. His job was to travel around to customers and service their office equipment. I used to tease him and say what he really had in the bag was a feather duster to provide the service required by the preventive maintenance contract.

In a few months we grew to know one another very well through telephone conversations. We could talk for hours. Ours was definitely something more than a casual friendship. There was a song popular at that time entitled "Mr. Wonderful, That's You." I felt the composer had written it just for me to describe my feelings for Wes. I had no idea what lay ahead for us, but I knew he was wonderful.

I had never thought about living anywhere else, but we moved several times as Wes climbed his ladder from service technician to president of Lanier Business Products. After we were married on February 2, 1957, we remained in Baton Rouge only seven months. Wes was promoted to sales along with service and we relocated to the Gulf Coast of Mississippi. He ran the business out of our home. The back bedroom of our small house became his office and service center. I answered the telephone for him, sent direct mail, and helped keep his records.

3

We had two daughters, and two years later were transferred to Augusta, Georgia. There Wes became a manager while remaining a salesman. We were excited over the prospect of his having an office downtown. There Wes earned his, and the company's, first incentive trip. We'd never dreamed of such an exciting adventure—a week in Acapulco! There have been many, many trips with Lanier since. My parents kept Jamey and Kandy and our new addition, Wesley.

Three years later we moved back to Baton Rouge when Wes became a full-fledged manager of a sizable region stretching from Beaumont, Texas through north Louisiana to Baton Rouge. It was unusual for a man to return as manager to an area where he had been a service technician. Wes worked the long, hard hours that have been his trademark. He probably learned more through on-the-job training there than in any other part of his career. In that role he tasted both the edge of failure and the joy of success and gained greatly from it.

Juli Anna, our fourth child, was one year old when in 1966 the company moved us to the home office in Atlanta, Georgia. Wes was promoted to vice president and sales manager (one of two). Wes became vice president/national sales manager in 1972, and in 1977, twenty-two years after taking that *temporary* job, became president of Lanier Business Products. The rest of his career has been spent in this city. Long ago we began to call it home.

Having been with the same company for so many years, Wes feels a great deal of loyalty to Lanier and to its name. Even when Harris Corporation bought Lanier in 1983, Wes retained his title of president, which pleased him very much. The company was called Harris/Lanier.

4

Four years later, the corporation made him president/CEO of Harris/3M Document Products, a joint venture of Harris and 3M. It was a great promotion and a happy-sad time for us at the thought of leaving these roots put down thirty-two years ago.

Another of Wes's dreams came to fruition in July 1989. The Harris Corporation bought 3M's interest in Harris/3M Document Products, combined it with the old Lanier and named the combination Lanier Worldwide, Inc. with Wes as president/CEO. Now he would head up a larger corporation with the name he loved. Guess what? It was the answer to a dream for me as well! Each rung of his ladder took **me** up also. *I climbed each rung with him. Within myself I felt as though I, too, had received a promotion.* My sincere desire is that you, too, will find such comraderie with your husband as I eventually found.

The Lord knew the whole picture for us, Wes and Bernadine were a good fit. At nineteen I thought little about the components of a good fit. My emotions played an important role in my decision. I was ecstatically in love.

A few years ago I listened as Wes shared at a church. He had been with Lanier only two months when Mr. Lanier called him in to request that he move to Louisiana. He went home to discuss it with his parents. He was torn. His girlfriend was in Georgia, he had that good looking red and white Chevrolet Bel-Air, and his circumstances were quite comfortable as they were. His parents' counsel was: Go where your employer wants you if you intend to get ahead. Wes immediately returned to his boss and accepted. At the time he didn't realize the guidance from the Lord given through his parents. Then Wes said something I hadn't heard before—"God was already getting a little Cajun girl ready to be my wife." About the time Wes graduated from college, I accepted Christ as my personal Savior.

Looking back, it is evident to both of us that I was chosen to help Wes become all God wanted him to be—a husband who is known in the gates!

2
The Way We Were

$\mathcal{T}$ he new young girl at the office was blonde, attractive, and efficient. I liked her quite well, but as time passed it became more and more difficult. I felt good about myself and our decision that I should stay at home. I was proud of the job I did taking care of our home and the children, but my secure feeling drained away as Wes spoke more frequently about the girl, implying that she was more efficient and necessary to the smooth running of the office every day. His complimentary remarks made me *feel* compared and inadequate. Wes spent a great deal of time at the office, more than at home. Consequently, I began to feel she was playing a more important role in his life than I.

He had an appointment in a nearby city, and I was expecting our third child at any time. Because we didn't have a second car and no close friends nearby, I asked, "What will I do if I go into labor?" He answered as though he had never thought of it as a problem, "Well, you know how to call a taxi, don't you?"

The doctor agreed to induce labor so we could have the baby while my parents were in town. Wes had gone home in the evening; he was tired and had to work the next day. The baby finally made it into the world in the early morning and I was ecstatic to have a little boy join our two girls. I could hardly wait for Wes to return to the hospital. I had encouraged him to go home, but at the same time I wanted very badly for him to stay with me. Business-minded man that he was, he had decided to get some sleep. Bursting with joy, I anticipated approval and expressions of gratitude when he learned we had a son. Anyone could see that he was very pleased, but he didn't say a word. "I thought you might thank me for giving you a son," I said. "You know who determines the sex of a baby, don't you?" was his practical response.

We were moving to another city. It never occurred to Wes to ask for a delay so we could sell our house. Off he went, leaving me to wrap up our affairs. Days and then weeks dragged by with no sale. In spite of having the children to care for and the house to keep ready for viewing at a moment's notice, I felt lonely and isolated. He seldom called or wrote. Even though I knew he was very busy in his new territory, I struggled emotionally with being left and seemingly forgotten.

We stood at the kitchen door with a strong emotional tug-of-war taking place. I was all but physically restraining Wes to keep him from leaving that late afternoon. I couldn't believe he was really going. It was my birthday; birthdays were important to me, and besides I was tired of being left behind. He insisted the business dinner with a prospective salesman and his wife was of far greater importance. I just couldn't understand why he hadn't planned to take me along. I begged and cried and asked him please to stay, but he coldly closed the door on my feelings and left me standing there all alone.

Weary of waiting for him to be expressive, to act as though I was an important part of his life, I was in a constant emotional battle. Wes was not a verbally demanding person, but I sensed his expectations that I keep everything spotless. With so much responsibility, it was impossible to meet his unspoken standards. I was constantly working, cleaning, sewing, taking care of four children, being active in the church, and trying to look attractive for him. He hardly seemed to notice me in the way I desired. I realized compliments I often received from other men were beginning to be more and more important to me. One night I explained what I was going through, that his neglect was making me vulnerable to other men. I pleaded with him to wake up in our relationship. He looked at me intently as though he might be hearing me, but nothing changed.

I was excited with the opportunity to speak before a graduating class at the Atlanta School for the Deaf. At the same time, I was scared to death! It never occurred to me that Wes wouldn't be proud of me, and I was sure he'd want to tag along. But he had an option, and he took it—a not-so-important event to attend with business associates. As I drove to the school, I had to take my feelings and stuff them away. I felt lonely and unloved, a state I had grown familiar with over the years.

When I was alone with the children, my mind constantly turned over ways I might handle emergencies. What if there is a fire? What would I do if a burglar broke into the house? Other questions plagued my mind. Where is my husband right now? Is he with a group of customers and managers, some of whom might be attractive young women? Why doesn't he call me when he's gone so long? What can I do when he gets home to make things better? Why can't he love me as I love him? What's wrong with me?

Sometimes when my feelings were totally out of control and there seemed nowhere to turn, I thought of escape. Surely there is someone out there who would love me, who would care for me. The children would be as well off; they never see their father much any way. I could compete with a another woman; I could threaten her life or scratch her eyes out, but it's hard to compete with business.

After reading all the applicable books, trying all the miracle cures, weeping, begging, pleading, threatening, and feeling sorry for myself, reality hit! He was not going to change, certainly not through *my* efforts! Where do I turn now? How could I continue striving to help Wes be a success when his success was the very thing which separated us?

3

Known in the Gates

J set out to be the world's greatest wife, not realizing that changing Wes was an unspoken and unrecognized part of my plan. Several years later I recognized my plan and came to the obvious conclusion that I was a failure as an agent of change. That was not for me to do.

A friend who had tried to help me through the years kept presenting the same truth over and over. "Bernie," he said, "when you stand before the Lord, you stand **alone**." When I was reminded of it by the Holy Spirit, I began to understand what he meant. The Lord holds **me** accountable for **me**. There will be no "Well, Lord, if You had only changed my husband, my home, my circumstances, I could have been a good wife. . . ." The responsibility was and is mine **alone**!

The Scriptures are full of good information which I had never investigated regarding my role as a wife. When I realized I was not in control of changing my husband and our relationship, I began to learn everything I could about my responsibilities according to God's plan. In reading Proverbs 31, I looked carefully at verse 23 which says the woman's "husband is known in the gates." Men met and transacted business at the city gates. I realized it was definitely saying something to me. I had to ask myself, what do I have to do with Wes's success? Does what I am have anything to do with my husband being well known in the business world?

"Houses and riches are the inheritance from fathers, but a wise, understanding, *and* prudent wife is from the Lord" (Proverbs 19:14). "The heart of her husband trusts in her confidently *and* relies on and believes in her safely, so that he has no lack of *honest* gain or need of *dishonest* spoil" (Proverbs 31:11). Yes, the Scriptures convinced me—I definitely had a part in my husband's success! I had simply chosen the wrong part.

I later discovered another verse that really excited me. "But woman is the [expression of] man's glory (majesty, and preeminence)" (I Corinthians 11:7b). Many questions came to mind as I confronted this verse. When I stand and sit, go and speak, how does the impression I make reflect on my husband? Do people look at me and see him as a success—a husband who is known in the gates?

The concept of **being** a woman who could free Wes to be a success rather than looking to change him brought a great sense of peace. I felt a huge weight lift from my shoulders. When we finally allow God to do what only He can do and devote ourselves to the task to which He has called us, our burdens are always lighter.

I needed a clear goal to shoot for, a definition of success by which I could measure my progress. After all, if I was going to help Wes become something, I needed a clear idea of what I was going to help him become.

In defining success, I had to fight the temptation to make a wish list. I was tempted to say a successful husband is one who always comes home on time, plays with the children and puts them to bed, talks to me about his private thoughts and dreams, makes a comfortable salary, is deeply devoted to me. . . . Another woman's wish list may be different. It might include loving yard work, making *lots* of money, buying expensive gifts, or bringing flowers home in the evening.

The definition which I feel is Biblical and obtainable gave me a focus. I believe *a successful husband is engaged in work that gives him satisfaction and a sense of significance, maintains a good name and reputation, has a rich personal relationship with his wife and family, and is habitually all-out for God.* I had always wanted to be Wes's support team, to help him accomplish his goals. The problem was that I wanted a return on my devotion that involved changes in Wes and his behavior toward me.

I have often thought one of the nicest qualities about Wes was his desire to assist those around him. He seemed to love helping others excel. After I began to focus on **being** a Biblically defined successful wife and relinquished the desire to change him, I was delighted to see evidence in my own life of the same quality. I wanted to help him God's way! Every time he received a promotion, I saw it as my promotion as well. I felt I was an integral part of his rewards. If

13

you're in on someone's triumph, it contributes to your own personal success.

My dad was a common laborer. He was the most **uncommon**, common laborer I have ever known. Dad enjoyed his job and his co-workers. In a supervisory role, he worked alongside his men, believing it assured them of his support and gave them confidence that he would never ask them to do something he wouldn't or couldn't do. He had a wonderful relationship with his wife and daughter. As a child, when I thought of God as Father, I'm sure I thought of my dad so it was easy for me to trust God. What really counts is *not* what a man's vocation may be, but the man, himself, and his attitude about his work and family.

Your husband may own a filling station, be a plumber, work in a department store, be a minister, or an accountant. If it is the right job for him, he will be content with it. If he is not content, he needs to feel free to seek a job in which he will be challenged, interested, and excited. What he does is unimportant, but how he does it and how he feels about it are important. If he is performing his best and providing for his family, that is what's important. Making a change will most likely cost everyone in the family in some way. A wife and mother must be willing to make the sacrifices and let her husband know that she is.

She must face some tough questions: Am I actively involved in helping my husband on his job? Am I willing to give up changing him and concentrate instead on my own development? It may sound as though a man's success rests on his wife's delicate shoulders. There will be times of wanting to rebel. Remember, I know the feeling. For my part, I am learning, and by practicing what God has taught me, I have found heart peace. I'm content to be a woman, a wife, a mother, a grandmother, and who I am in Jesus.

A man's reputation follows him into every aspect of his life. Wes's desire has been to have a good name and reputation (Proverbs 21:1). He knows the requirements are simple. He must keep his word and have a clear conscience between himself and everyone with whom he comes in contact.

It's impossible to have everyone think well of us. There may be people who say things to your discredit. Your husband may be responsible for evaluating the performance of others, he may have to demote someone, or even fire someone. These are unpleasant happenings and sometimes the people involved will speak critically about him.

Others may be unable to deal with his role and standards. They may envy him or resent his accomplishments and abilities. Fortunately, he does not have to account for their reactions. Every individual is accountable for himself. Your husband's responsibility is for his own performance—did he do all he could to make things right?

Wes suffers emotionally when people respond improperly and turn their frustration on him. He is especially troubled by rejection. On a number of occasions someone whom he considered a friend has spoken harshly against him. Journalists have been critical or inaccurate in their articles about him. When Wes realizes his conversation or conduct was improper, he returns to the injured person to ask for forgiveness. For the sake of a good name and reputation, one must be ready to do so. Even those who disagree with you about issues will respect you.

The last thing a husband needs in such times of trial is a "helper meet" standing on the sidelines throwing stones with the crowd. We can't stop people from being critical of our husbands, but we can make sure that we are never part of the problem. We should instead be part of the solution, so look for ways you can help build your husband's good reputation.

"A rich personal relationship with wife and family" is the part of my definition that most people leave out when they discuss success. Because we want our men to be successful husbands and fathers, many of our relationships begin with attempts to change them. I have found that Wes responds much better to me when I am helping him, not trying to change him.

What is the difference? When I wanted to change Wes, it was usually in a way that was good for me. As I have shifted my focus, I find it easier to keep his best interests in mind. Consequently, he feels I'm working with him rather than against him. Semantics? No, it's a liberating attitude that does wonders for a marriage. It is what Paul meant when he said "Love . . . does not insist on its own rights . . ." (I Corinthians 13:5). Working to make your husband successful is love in action. Our selfish tendency is to seek our own happiness; our role according to God is just the opposite.

Your husband may not be a Christian. It doesn't in any way change your role or how you should respond to him. However, it should have a tremendous impact on your prayer life. Encourage your husband always and in all ways to focus his life on glorifying the Lord. The greatest encouragement is your own growth in the knowledge of the Lord and in obedience to His Word.

Wes and I have used and abused every principle in this book. I wish I could tell you that if you follow those which I share with you from the Word, you will get all you desire and perhaps expect. I wish I could tell you the result will be Mr. Ideal! I cannot, but I can assure you of one thing. As you begin to take God's principles and integrate them into your life, you will gain a heart peace which passes all understanding.

In helping your husband become what God wants him to be, something will happen to you. What do you need to relinquish? What responsibilities have you taken which are not yours? How can you deal with the frustration of unfulfilled dreams and expectations, neglect, or even rejection?

I pray that you will absorb each of these powerful principles and live by them. As you read, you may be tempted to skip over the Scripture passages. They are the basis of the principles, so surrender yourself to a teachable heart and read them carefully. Open the door for God to richly bless you and your marriage. You can be a Proverbial woman whose husband is known in the gates!

For God so greatly loved and dearly prized the world that He [even] gave up His only-begotten (unique) Son, so that whoever believes in (trusts, clings to, relies on) Him shall not perish—come to destruction, be lost—but have eternal (everlasting) life.

—John 3:16

4
His Work Was Not My Enemy

$\mathcal{I}$ don't know when I realized that Wes's work was not my enemy. My enemy was the world—television, movies, magazines, friends that convinced me of an inaccurate picture of life. I married believing my husband was going to be a certain way—a way I had imagined. My enemy was my flesh, which wanted him to be and act in the ways I chose. My enemy was Satan, who deceived me. I remained ignorant of the truth for a very long time. My problem was learning to be responsible for me, and responding and walking in the light of who I am in Christ. When I changed my thinking, I began to get a glimpse of how things should be. This is the secret of any woman being the successful wife of a successful husband. For all of us, there is an answer: **be** what you are, be accountable to the Lord, and leave the results to Him. That commitment is a pivotal step for every woman. It certainly was for me.

THE INITIAL STEP

One day I began teaching a new series of Bible studies at a neighborhood church. As is my custom, I interjected all during my lesson the words *born again*. A lady in one of the small group sessions left and wandered up and down the corridors. She wanted to ask someone how to be born again. When I learned about it, I prayed, "Thank you, Father, for this gentle reminder." I must never assume people know what I am talking about, so I must start at the beginning. Having accepted Christ as my personal Savior before I met Wes was the first milestone of my life—and for building our home. If you know the Lord, He will be the Rock, the foundation of your home, too.

You may have heard these expressions before: you can take a litter of kittens and raise them in an oven, but they never become cupcakes. You can take a horse and put him in your garage, and even after many years, he never becomes a car. A lot of us had parents who sent us to church every week, perhaps on a bus or with someone else. Maybe we had grandmothers who took us. Somehow or other, we were parked in a church, but never really came to know the Lord.

No matter how many years you have attended church and Bible classes, read good books, been a moral person, or identified yourself as a Christian, it is all in vain without having Christ in your heart and life. Satan has and will deceive many to believe they are spiritually secure when they are not. Most likely any woman reading this material is born again, but there might be one who may later wander up and down the corridors of her life looking for someone who could answer her question, I would like to be born again. Can you tell me how?

You may be thinking that you wouldn't be reading this now if you didn't know Jesus already. I would like to encourage you with a reminder. One day I was telling a friend about my experiences and realized that he not only knew and understood the truths I was sharing but probably had the same experiences long before I did. When I quickly apologized, he quoted Romans 10:17 and added, "Faith comes by hearing, so tell me again what I already know."

Knowing Jesus is the only way to have a relationship with God the Father. He said, "I am the Way and the Truth and the Life; no one comes to the Father except by (through) Me" (John 14:6). So it is not enough to believe in God. You must acknowledge that Jesus is the Lamb of God, His only begotten Son. All the Old Testament sacrifices were only a foreshadowing of what Jesus did for you and me. He died, was buried, and was raised that you and I might be resurrected and live with Him for eternity. We must have Jesus, not only for our future life, but to have an abundant life right now.

Let's settle the issue. "Behold, now is the day of salvation" (II Corinthians 6:2c)! There will never be a better time than right now to be saved. If you have never made this commitment, you have the privilege of receiving Him today. If you have never made this choice, you need to invite Him into your heart. He promises He will come in (Revelation 3:20) and never leave. ". . . [I will] not, [I will] not in any degree leave you helpless, *nor* forsake *nor* let [you] down, [relax my hold on you]—assuredly not" (Hebrews 13:6)!

The Lord gives a measure of faith to each and every person. You have the choice of directing your measure toward any object you

21

choose. For you, it may have been education, looks, prestige, career, husband, or an organized church. Salvation comes when you redirect your focus of faith and change your mind about Jesus. Changing your mind about Jesus is your responsibility. That is salvation repentance. Behavioral repentance comes afterward. "And I am convinced *and* sure of this very thing, that He Who began a good work in you will continue until the day of Jesus Christ—right up to the time of His return—developing [that good work] and perfecting and bringing it to full completion in you" (Philippians 1:6). He is the One who does the empowering so your behavior will come into harmony with His will.

If you feel an urging in your heart, the Holy Spirit is speaking to you and gently knocking at the door of your heart. Please answer His personal invitation **today**. You must willingly open your heart, saying, "Lord Jesus, I need You. I receive You as my Lord and Savior. Thank you for saving me from the penalty and power of sin by the shedding of Your blood on Calvary."

Wes and I have often been reminded of the Scripture about the foolish man who builds his house upon the sand and the wise man who builds his house upon the rock. Many have tried to build a Christian life but did not begin with the firm foundation of the born-again experience. Many have been parked in a church and have tried to act like Christians, but found it fruitless and unstable. Be the wise (wo)man. Build your house upon the Rock of the Lord Jesus Christ. When the storms come, which they will, the house will not fall.

KNOWING WHO YOU ARE

Wes told me once that I was the most spiritual girl he ever dated, but I did not feel that way. Later I came to realize that I truly had been saved by God's grace but was attempting to live my Christian life by self-effort.

If you have been born again, are you really different? "Therefore if any person is (ingrafted) in Christ, the Messiah, he is (a new creature altogether,) a new creation, the old (previous moral and spiritual condition) has passed away. Behold, the fresh *and* new has come!" (II Corinthians 5:17).

Where is the previous moral and spiritual condition? It's not here any more! What good news for me. I had thought it was ever-present.

Why wasn't the change obvious? I had been a Christian for several years and had been **trying** to be different. I knew I should be, but I was failing. You may be born again and not **feel** or believe or act it. You may not **know** what has changed. Understanding took me quite awhile; then I learned what God said. What wonderful news!

I am different! "I have been crucified with Christ—[in Him] I have shared His crucifixion; it is no longer I who live, but Christ, the Messiah, lives in me, and the life I now live in the body I live by faith—by adherence to *and* reliance on *and* [complete] trust—in the Son of God, Who loved me and gave Himself up for me" (Galatians 2:20).

What do you think this verse means? "Are you ignorant of the fact that all of us who have been baptized into Christ Jesus were baptized into His death?" (Romans 6:3).

So where were we when Jesus died? "We were buried therefore with Him by the baptism into death, so that just as Christ was raised from the dead by the glorious [power] of the Father so we too might habitually live and behave . . ." (Romans 6:4).

How? Is this Scripture speaking about our experience? "So we too might habitually live *and* behave in newness of life." It sounds experiential. We share His death, His burial, and His resurrection and we are freed from the power of sin. "Now if we died with Christ we believe that we shall also **live** with Him" (Romans 6:8, emphasis added).

We will live differently! What a discovery! My thinking began to catch up with God's truth.

A born-again can struggle for years as I did because of ignorance and unbelief. The conflict between your feelings, actions, and thinking about how a Christian should act can make you feel like a hypocrite. If this has been your experience, perhaps you haven't learned to be a faith-walker. I had not, but I wanted to.

Satan has a definition of hypocrite that many of you have bought—acting different from what you *feel*. It's a lie, yet every assertiveness class and self-esteem-building group would have you believe it. They say if you feel angry, show it; don't lie about it. Don't be deceptive—act like you feel. When someone speaks of kindness, say that you don't feel like being kind. To forgive would be unthinkable if you don't feel forgiving. Don't listen to Satan's messengers! Remember the reputation of feelings—they are not reliable. Sometimes they are accurate; sometimes dead wrong, so you cannot depend on them for guidance. You must depend only upon the Word of God and reject the lies of the deceiver and the words of men.

I had been a hypocrite by not acting like God said I was. God's definition of hypocrisy is **acting** different from what you **are**—which according to Romans 6:6 is born again and a **new creation**. When you **act** like the old person, you are being a hypocrite. God would have you **act** like what you **are**. You must know who and what God says you are.

Many Christians believe "I am just a dirty old sinner saved by grace." A born-again **was** a lost sinner, but has become a blood-washed believer, a saint who may occasionally sin—saved by God's grace. It is an entirely different perspective. If you get up in the morning thinking you are just a dirty old sinner who happens to be saved by grace, what will you do all day? Most likely you'll sin and won't even be surprised. Saints should be surprised when they sin. What an exciting truth! Many happy changes began to happen in my life when I recognized it.

Unless you live according to God's definition of who you are in Christ, you'll easily slip into wrong actions, just as I did. Wrong actions come from wrong thinking. It is easy to believe what you **feel** or perceive as truth rather than to believe God. The deceiver was keeping me from it. I was living a defeated life; my feelings and incorrect thinking dominated my decisions and actions. We must examine our thinking in the light of God's Word.

Years ago Wes and I taught college students at our church. We "adopted" a precious young girl named Kristi. She was from Missouri and far away from relatives and friends. The Lord used our pastor to encourage us to get more intimately involved with individual students and we did. Kristi became part of our family, and after many years she and her family are still an important part of our lives. Kristi spent many weekends at our house. She was a lovely person; however, she did have a weight problem. I wasn't a help because I enjoyed cooking so much, especially elaborate meals on weekends.

As Kristi grew in the Lord, she began to discipline herself. She didn't go on a crash diet, but steadily lost weight. Some time later when she was getting married, I gave a lingerie shower for her. As we designed the invitation, she wrote down her sizes which she stated as twelve to fourteen. By this time she was a size six to eight. What was her problem? Do you think she was feeling good about herself? She was a slender lady but still saw herself as overweight. She was still dressing herself as though she were large.

You may be a saint who is living spiritually as Kristi was physically. If you think you are the same as you **were**, that's the way you will live, instead of living like what you **are**! You must do as Kristi did. Stand in front of a full-length mirror (the Word of God) and see all of what you are. Don't let this example confuse you. I'm not referring to your physical weight but to living out what God says you are, not pretending or play acting.

Manley Beasley's workbook taught me about faith: faith is counting so, what is not so, that it may be so, because God said so. Whether you feel it or not, whether it looks true or not, count it to be so because God says it! You must recognize that you are not living by feelings but by faith. Acknowledge to God that you believe Him, that you are a new creation. Then you can and will "habitually live and behave in newness of life."

RECOGNIZE THE ENEMY

Satan is constantly attempting to make the born-again believe what is false. The way to find out what you truly are is to be very familiar with the Word. Don't believe negative things others tell you; don't believe what Satan tells you; believe what the Word tells you. If what you hear is negative, accusing, and opposite of what the Word of God says, you can be sure the source is the deceiver. "So be subject to God—stand firm against the devil; resist him and he will flee from you" (James 4:7). "For he is a liar [himself] and the father of lies *and of all that is false*" (John 8:44c).

Satan hates Christ and those who have Christ. Satan does not want you to be who and what you are in Christ. Submit to the Lord, rebuke the enemy verbally, aloud, and walk in freedom.

What a remarkable, exciting, freeing milestone in my life—and only a beginning. Many smaller benchmarks came later and are occurring daily, but it all began when I saw myself as my heavenly Father says I am. It continues as I daily recognize the enemy. Each day seems to bring more revelation and freedom as I accept truth as living reality. When life becomes topsy-turvy and I **feel** confused and frustrated, I know I have temporarily forgotten who I truly am—a new creation and a daily victor.

KNOW YOURSELF

Then came the milestone of realizing who I am as a woman. Identifying myself as the woman God wants me to be has been not only freeing but fun! I heard David McLaughlin speak. He used some meaningful dialogue to focus on a most important issue—men and women are *different* from one another. Look at the creation of the sexes—we were even made from different material. The female was sculptured by the Lord from flesh and blood. He used dirt to make the male. That should give us our first clue—very different building material. Men and women are distinct from each other in many ways. Recognizing the *difference,* we can more readily accept that our husbands and other men will not respond in the same way we do.

I needed to understand my role as a wife, and the Lord was faithful in teaching me. Genesis 2:18 speaks of making woman "a helper meet." You need to understand what that means if you have a heart to be what God says you are. A helpmeet means someone who is suitable, adapted, completing to her husband. A man is not made to adapt to you—the exact opposite of what the feminists are telling us today. Their wrong thinking is overflowing into the Christian family and affecting our own families in a negative way.

You, the wife, the helpmeet, are the one to be suitable, adapted, completing. You may have some difficulty in accepting that description. I certainly did. Even now in the middle of enjoying who I am, I still struggle. Recognizing and accepting that this is the way God made you and me will help us get excited about His plan. Functioning according to His design will bring the highest pleasure and satisfaction.

Adam called his wife Eve which means life spring. Woman can give life, produce babies, but she is not limited to physical birth. Barren women can have many spiritual children—they can give life. As we share Christ with others, we are sharing the message of life. We can give a taste of life to others in many ways such as working with children and giving them hope and encouragement. It is one of our greatest privileges.

When I first became interested in the meaning of names, one of the few I could remember was the meaning of John. I was at an elementary school helping teachers check students' eyes. Every time a small fellow named John came into the room I shared with him the meaning of his name. One boy who was much taller than the rest of his class came in and stood near me as I asked quietly, "John, do you know what your name means?" He wrinkled his brow and replied after a moment's hesitation, "Toilet?"

What do you think was happening inside John? What about his self-acceptance? I had never made a connection between the name John and a toilet, but this little boy had. As soon as I could recover from his shocking remark, I said, "Your name means God's gracious gift!" What a wonderful change came over his face. I believe I gave him a touch of life. That is something I can do for every person I touch in my sphere of influence, and you can, too! Giving life in such ways is not only right, but it is also fulfilling. If you are free to be what God made you to be, it will be one of your heart's desires. It is a womanly quality.

Unfortunately, one of Eve's nicest traits led her into trouble. She saw the fruit and it looked good. Women like themselves and their surroundings to look good. If they are **free,** that is! A couple spent time in jungle camp on a missionary training program. The husband joked about his wife trying to make diapers into curtains for their lean-to. She wanted her surroundings to look good.

Many times the love of beauty leads us girls into financial stress. We see things we believe could enhance our beauty or that of our surroundings, and we weaken. We love beauty and we like to create it. God created this very special quality in women and we need to use it but *not abuse it.*

One young woman who was experiencing financial bondage needed a little encouragement. I invited her to our home for some one-on-one fellowship. During this special time I discovered something important about her: she had not felt good about herself as a woman. She was overweight and her hairstyle was unflattering. She seemed to have no interest in taking the time or making the effort to look her best. Beginning a new diet, a softer hairstyle, and the application of makeup gave me the clue that something was going on inside. As we talked she told me about being sexually abused as a child. She told me that she had never wanted to be pretty. The experience had blocked what she was! Through forgiveness, the Lord had intervened and was giving her a clearer picture of who she was. Now freed, she was creating beauty; she was becoming what God created her to be.

ACCEPT YOURSELF AND FORGET YOURSELF

Knowing who you are is important. The next step is to fully accept that person. Instead of comparing yourself to someone else, thank God for making you exactly the way you are. Go a step further. Give thanks for the rest—your talents, even what you consider lack of talents, your temperament, heritage, present circumstances. Accept yourself with thanksgiving. "Thank [God] in everything—no matter what the circumstances may be, be thankful and give thanks; for this is the will of God for you [who are] in Christ Jesus [the Revealer and Mediator of that will]" (I Thessalonians 5:18).

You need to love yourself—not the flesh, the old self, or the old sin nature—but who you are in Christ. In the principle of loving your neighbor as yourself, that assumption is made (Luke 10:27). If you don't think well of yourself, how will you view another? You must love yourself before you can love anyone else, and the Lord is your Enabler. Once you know yourself, accept yourself, give thanks for yourself, and love yourself, you are free to forget about yourself and to serve others!

There is nothing like freedom! When you're preparing to attend an important event, you carefully select your dress and the suitable accessories. You take pains to be well-groomed in all details, including hose, shoes, purse, jewelry, hair, and nails. Your thoughts are full of yourself during your preparations. When you're satisfied with the results, you are free to concentrate on others; you can forget about yourself. Both the *choice* and the responsibility are yours.

Let's summarize the major milestones, each one of them necessary to becoming the kind of wife the Lord wants you to be. First, you must be born again. Second, to be a successful born-again, you must know who you are in Christ. Third, recognize the enemy. Fourth, come to understand who you are as a woman and as a wife. You are different from your husband. Fifth, accept yourself and love yourself so you will know how to love and serve others, especially your husband.

What therefore God has united—joined together—let not man separate or divide.

—Mark 10:9

5

Is This Forever?!

*E*very time we hit a bump in the road of our marriage, the thought came. Every time I felt hurt, discouragement, or anger, the thought came. Get out of here; you'll be free and he can't hurt you anymore! Books, teachers, counselors, and even preachers often suggest loop-holes. I was looking for escape but also wanted God's peace. I found I couldn't have both. I was in this for keeps!

Why is permanency of marriage so important? Why is it a forever deal? Why is it so important to those who follow after us that our marriage is stable and that we obviously love one another? First, our children will know there is one thing you can really count on in this life. Second, the world will see that our marriage is a beautiful earthly picture of Heaven. Third, it is a witness to the world of the dependability and reliability of our heavenly Father.

The permanence of marriage from God's point of view is directly opposed to the current world view of marriage. You must look carefully at your *beliefs* about marriage. Please answer truthfully—what do you really believe?

Is marriage a God-ordained institution? God our Creator determined that man needed a companion. Immediately after woman's creation, God established this special relationship, that a man should leave father and mother and cleave to his wife.

> Now the Lord God said, It is not good [sufficient, satisfactory] that the man should be alone; I will make him a helper meet (suitable, adapted, completing) for him. . . . And the rib *or* part of his side which the Lord God had taken from the man, He built up *and* made into a woman and brought her to the man. Then, Adam said, This [creature] is now bone of my bones and flesh of my flesh. She shall be called Woman . . . Therefore a man shall leave his father and his mother and shall become united *and* cleave to his wife, and they shall become one flesh. Genesis 2:18-24

Has God designed a structure for marriage and given a complete description of each role? In Ephesians and Titus, Paul outlines the role of each family member and the responsibilities assigned to each one.

34

Wives, be subject—be submissive and adapt yourselves—to your own husbands as [a service] to the Lord. For the husband is head of the wife as Christ is the Head of the church, Himself the Savior of [His] body. As the church is subject to Christ, so let wives also be subject in everything to their husbands. Husbands, love your wives, as Christ loved the church and gave Himself up for her. . . . Even so husbands should love their wives as [being in a sense] their own bodies. He who loves his own wife loves himself. . . . For this reason a man shall leave his father and his mother. . . . However, let each man of you (without exception) love his wife as [being in a sense] his very own self; and let the wife see that she respects *and* reverences her husband—that she notices him, regards him, honors him, prefers him, venerates and esteems him; and that she defers to him, praises him, and loves and admires him exceedingly. (Ephesians 5:22-33)

So that they will wisely train the young women . . . to love their husbands and their children; To be self-controlled, chaste, homemakers, good-natured (kind-hearted), adapting *and* subordinating themselves to their husbands. (Titus 2:4,5a)

Has God given loopholes to terminate marriage? Scripture can be used to give a husband or wife justification to break their marriage vows, but other verses should prepare a wife for the unalterable character of her vows from God's perspective. These verses eliminate the loopholes. Let no one tear apart by his own efforts or understanding what has been put together by vows to a holy God.

> And the two shall become one flesh, so that they are no longer two, but one flesh. What therefore God has united—joined together—let not man separate *or* divide. (Mark 10:8,9)

> For [instance] a married woman is bound by law to her husband as long as he lives. (Romans 7:2a)

One excuse used for divorce is the number of offenses of the husband. Jesus said we are to forgive without limit on the number of times and without conditions about the offense.

> Then Peter came up to Him and said, Lord, how many times may my brother sin against me, and I forgive him *and* let it go? As many as up to seven times? Jesus answered him, I tell you, not up to seven times, but seventy times seven! . . . So also My heavenly Father will deal with every one of you, if you do not freely forgive your brother from your heart *his offenses*. (Matthew 18:21,22,35)

God hates divorce and Moses allowed it only because of the hardness of hearts.

Is it lawful *and* right to dismiss *and* repudiate *and* divorce one's wife for any *and* every cause? . . . Why then did Moses command [us] to give a certificate of divorce, and thus to dismiss *and* repudiate a wife? He said to them, Because of the hardness (stubbornness and perversity) of your hearts Moses permitted you to dismiss *and* repudiate *and* divorce your wives; but from the beginning it has not been so [ordained]. (Matthew 19:3b-8)

For the Lord, the God of Israel says: I hate divorce *and* marital separation. (Malachi 2:16a)

Should a woman leave her husband? Paul makes a wife's options very clear—she should not leave her husband, but if she does, she has only two choices.

But to the married [people] I give charge, not I but the Lord, that the wife is not to separate from her husband. But if she does [separate from and divorce him], let her remain single or else be reconciled to her husband. And [I charge] the husband [also] that he should not put away *or* divorce his wife. (I Corinthians 7:10-11)

Scholars have debated over the interpretation of the verses which seem to say there are reasons you may divorce. If your commitment is limited by those excuses, you are shortchanging your vows. Your

37

vows, along with your commitment to forgive all things at all times, do away with the arguments of scholars with no furthur debate.

As I speak to young people considering marriage, my question is, "Are you willing to walk into a room with no other doors and no windows and have the door sealed behind you?" If so, you are prepared for marriage. If not, don't bother. Why involve another life in a limited and conditional commitment?

When you marry conditionally, you are not entering marriage with your whole heart; no matter how small or seemingly insignificant the reservations, your marriage is already in jeopardy. The enemy will apply pressure to the areas of weakness.

Before marriage is the time to filter your thinking about marriage through the Word of God. After the wedding you will often experience circumstances which reveal conditional thinking. You may say, "My experience does not line up with God's Word. My situation is an exception. It is impossible. No one understands how difficult it is. I cannot forgive this particular thing. When I said 'for better or for worse,' I had no idea what worse really meant. My spouse changed after we were married." Experience may alter your thinking, but it can never change the Word of God. Regardless of experience, yours or a loved one's, your thinking needs to line up with Scripture.

If you are married, you are married to exactly the right man for you! Often we get into a situation without consulting the Lord, or we ignore His urgings and go ahead with our plan. Then we plead, "Lord, please bless this mess." We might even have the audacity to ask, "Lord, why are You permitting this? Why did You allow this to happen to me?"

So you are not happy with your marriage? Start right where you are. Confess if you did not abide by the Lord's guidance or your parents' counsel. Make restitution with everyone involved. Read the Word and correct your thinking about marriage. Then launch into a whole new program. May the Lord bless you richly as you reach out for God's best where you are right now!

Lord, I surrender my husband to You, my assumed right to change him, and my assumed responsibility to make everything work out right. I surrender my reliance upon me, my reasoning, and my resources. I surrender to Your design, Your plan for my marriage. Make of me all You want me to be. I only assume *my* responsibilities as designated by You. Give me the wisdom to know what they are and the courage to fulfill them.

Praise the Lord that He showed me Truth and I chose His way. First, I look at my children who would have paid the price for my going my own selfish way, and I praise Him. Second, I think of those who have watched our relationship and rejoice that they see at least in part a picture of Heaven. Third, as I share my experiences, I can boast in the Lord Who made it possible. I praise our heavenly Father for His dependability and reliability to enable and empower me, just as He will enable and empower you.

But let it be the inward adorning and beauty of the hidden person of the heart, with the incorruptible and unfading charm of a gentle and peaceful spirit, which (is not anxious or wrought up, but) is very precious in the sight of God.

—I Peter 3:4

6

The Hidden Motivator

$\mathcal{A}$ woman can change her husband's mood from "Is it really worth it?" to "She can make it all seem worthwhile!" without a word. All it takes is demonstrating a gracious attitude toward him, maybe with a quiet smile, a nod of approval, or an admiring glance. You know what the hidden motivator is—your attitude! Are you due for an attitude check-up? How does yours measure up to God's standard?

AN ATTITUDE OF CONTENTMENT

You may look to your husband to build up your confidence with frequent compliments. Maybe he doesn't allow you to express yourself verbally or show you physical affection. Perhaps you need him to take care of home repairs, cars, or even children. Whatever the insecurity or need, I know you are looking for an answer. Just as you think your husband is responsible to meet your needs, I was looking to Wes for mine.

I was unhappy and discontent, and I reminded myself of a toddler just learning to walk. When he falls he looks for someone to blame it on. Most likely he will swat at the nearest small guy or cry to mommy. We all have a little toddler inside still struggling to walk. The old pattern of wanting someone else to meet our needs or blame when things don't go our way is difficult to give up.

I thought I had a great need to feel loved by my husband. I was sure I had to feel loved by him to be secure. All of us girls want to be secure, and we try to find security by different means. Some might mention a larger home, designer clothes, a huge diamond, having four children, or not having any. A wife may link all her needs to her husband—if he were only, . . . if he made more money, was more sensitive, attentive, helpful. If only he would change. When you place unmet expectations on your husband, no matter how you try to conceal it, he will sense your discontent and feel inadequate or confused.

Once a wife begins to focus on such things, she loses sight of what God wants her to be and what He says she is. We must guard against having the wrong focus. As Christians, we are to look to the Lord Jesus Christ to meet our needs. Many times He will work through our husbands. Then again, He may not. By simply placing the fulfillment of our needs on the Lord and looking to Him to put proper desires in our hearts (Psalm 37:4-5), we can begin to project an attitude of contentment to our husbands.

AN ATTITUDE OF TRUST

A wife must trust the Lord and her husband to be responsible for the marriage relationship. Often magazines give an opportunity to grade husbands and relationships. Perhaps your pastor preaches a good sermon on family relationships, and you take more notice of your husband's responsibility than your own. Through seminars, courses, and books you can draw up a plan with all the pieces arranged to result in the perfect family. And, of course, you think you must oversee the process. After all, if you don't, who will?

Dear sweet lady, you are believing the devil's lie. You are not in charge of your relationship with your husband, and it is not your responsibility. You are accountable for one person and her attitude—**you**.

I had known for a long time that woman is the responder and man is the leader, but it has been exciting to experience that concept. When Wes and I quarreled, I'd decide to be cool and aloof. Later, with only a small gesture of tenderness and affection from Wes, I'd feel myself soften and lean toward him. The Lord gave us the model in the church's relationship with Christ. He is the Head; the church, the responder. I was not accountable for my husband's actions, responses, or role. In responding, I was responsible and accountable for me.

Several years ago, the Lord showed me this truth, and I didn't know what to do about it. One day I approached Wes with my thoughts, "The Lord has shown me something and I am going to say it the best I can. Please try to understand 'between the lines.' I've never been told how to do this, so I have to communicate my way.

I've been acting responsible for our marriage and for our relationship. I am no longer going to do it." The expression on his face told me that I had done a poor job of getting across what I was experiencing. I repeated, "I am not going to be responsible any more." "Are you trying to tell me you are not going to be a good wife?" he asked. "No, I am not making myself clear. I will continue to study the Word and try to be everything God wants me to be, including being the very best wife I can be, but I will discontinue assuming responsibility for our relationship."

I wouldn't advise you to say such a thing to your husband unless the Lord really moves you to do so. I am a verbally expressive person, and it's difficult for me to hold back. For some temperaments and gifts, speaking out may not be a need. Perhaps all you need to do is confess to the Lord that you have been acting responsible for your marriage relationship. Give it to the Lord and accept the responsibility for *your response* to and *your attitude* toward your husband.

Later Wes attended a seminar, and something said there inspired him to share with me, "Giving up the responsibility for our marriage was one of the wisest things you ever did." Even though I thought I had blown it, my husband turned it over in his mind after our conversation. He read between the lines and understood what I was trying to say.

"But let it be the inward adorning *and* beauty of the hidden person of the heart, with the incorruptible *and* unfading charm of a gentle and peaceful spirit which (is not anxious or wrought up, but) is very precious in the sight of the God" (I Peter 3:4). How do you meet your husband at the door? Peacefully or do you dump on him all the problems of the day? I can assure you, if you will allow the Lord to manifest these Biblical qualities through you to your husband, it will be precious in his sight! and the Lord's!

When you decide to get with God's program, keep a watchful eye on your husband. Regardless of past tensions, clashes, or disharmony, the lines in his face will soften; and you'll see a mellow expression in his eyes. You will have God's heart peace as you commit yourself to becoming the kind of woman He wants you to be and assuming *only* the responsibility He gives to you. Your husband will feel your new attitude of trust in him as you trust in the Lord.

AN ATTITUDE OF LOVE FREELY GIVEN

The love of a Godly woman is a strong force in a man's life. To allow your husband to leave home without the confidence of your love is like having an itch in the middle of your back that you cannot reach. It is not a comfortable condition. I have always wanted Wes to leave our home knowing he can be confident of my love and support. I want him to feel good about himself because someone else feels good about him.

When your husband goes to work he should feel armed for the day. I wrote a little rhyme as a teenager, and one line has stayed in my memory. "When that girl makes eyes at you, tell her you have a love that's true." Many women are making eyes at men today. They have no regard for a wedding ring. I would like my husband to feel he has someone who loves him true everyday when he is away from me. Every time some woman gives him a compliment (and you can be sure they will), I want him to think smugly, Bernie already said that.

Love freely given is not conditional upon treatment or circumstances. Love freely given is powerful in the life of the receiver *and the giver*.

AN ATTITUDE OF SERVICE

Perhaps you serve all the time, but what about your attitude? No one may know you have a bad one except the Lord and your husband. They definitely know. Your husband doesn't notice the wonderful things you do for him; he probably isn't even aware of your deeds of service. Sometimes other men see how we minister to our husbands and think we are great, but they don't see our attitude. Your husband may seem ungrateful because he senses your attitude. Satan can readily use this contrast.

By serving your husband you aid him in learning to think of others. Then service becomes a part of his success. No matter what his job is, he can always find someone to serve. "Through love you should serve one another" (Galatians 5:13b). "Whoever desires to be great among you must be your servant, and whoever wishes to be most important *and* first in rank among you must be the slave of all" (Mark 10:43b-44).

Serving your husband as one who intelligently chooses to serve and *gladly* serves will greatly affect both you, the giver, and your husband, the receiver. It is a privilege when done by choice and with an attitude of gladness.

AN ATTITUDE OF GRATEFULNESS

One day Wes came in and said, "Honey, something very interesting happened to me today. A woman made an appointment with me, and our conversation was quite a surprise."

"Mr. Cantrell," she said, "I came to tell you how much I appreciate my job. I enjoy my work so much, and I simply wanted to tell you that I appreciate having an employer like you." You can guess his response. That she received his undivided attention grabbed my undivided attention.

Sometime later I wrote this letter to Wes at the office:

My dear husband,

The Lord gently reminded me again this morning of this note I have intended to write to you for several weeks. This is actually a thank-you note. I want to say officially thanks for my job.

Thank you not only for giving me this job, but allowing me to keep it. Thank you for never acting as though you would like to replace me even though I am certain there were times. . . .

Thanks for a lovely building to work in and on, a nice car to carry out my duties with, all the latest equipment in good shape, nice companions to rub shoulders with, a sexy bed partner, nice clothes, nice trips, and so countless many fringe benefits. But most of all, thanks for your commitment to me, your love and faithfulness, and love and commitment to the Lord and your growing fellowship with Him.

I love you, Wes

Bernie

When I talked with him years later about the letter, he said it was tucked away in his dresser. He has kept few treasures so carefully.

Have you become so busy and distracted by negatives that you forget to be sensitive and grateful to your husband? We need to check our focus often and switch it from *feeling* to *being* what we are.

Gratitude is a big morale booster. It's a great motivator for your husband to excel not only in his vocation but also in his relationship with you. Wives, we must wake up. We are living in a time when society no longer puts pressure on people to be faithful in their marriages. That pressure comes only from the Lord and is often ignored or resisted. There are women on the prowl, and they seek your husband's attention. The way to help him resist any snare is not by jealousy or catty criticism but by meeting his innermost needs. You can strengthen him by verbally expressing your gratitude and radiating an attitude of gratefulness.

AN ATTITUDE OF CHEERFULNESS

The Lord expects two kinds of responses from us regarding obedience—**willful** obedience (choosing God's ways) and having a **right attitude** about it. Psalm 100:2 is only one of many references to a right attitude in obedience, "Serve the Lord with gladness," with joy—with emotion. Another example is tithing, "for God loves (that is, He takes pleasure in, prizes above other things, and is unwilling to abandon or to do without) a cheerful (joyous, prompt-to-do-it) giver—whose heart is in his giving" (II Corinthians 9:7b).

Obey with emotion, one that you can choose. If you are happy only when getting your own way, you have never been truly happy. Are you dependant upon self-satisfaction to feel good about your marriage? When you struggle over something with your husband, you may be doing it for the wrong reason—fighting to get your way. Even if you win, it never seems to satisfy. Make the right choice—give it up. A woman is created to be suitable, adapted, and completing to her husband. Fulfillment cannot come outside of God's design.

As he was leaving for work one day, Wes told me he wanted me to give up a weekly Bible class without explaining his reasons. I didn't like it at all and still remember the strong emotion I felt—the nerve of him! After I had fretted around the house for quite awhile, the Lord spoke to me in my spirit.

"Do you mean what you've been saying?" He asked. I had thought I did, and giving up the class was not a terrible struggle so what was my problem? Within minutes I saw the truth. I could hardly wait for Wes to arrive at the office so I could call him. As soon as he answered, I told him I realized my intent of being right and winning the argument had become my focus. God was using my husband to give me new direction and I almost missed it by defending my rights. My priorities had too quickly gotten out of order.

Choosing an attitude of cheerfulness when we do what we ought to do is rewarding. It's pleasant for your husband, and you reap the personal benefit of a good feeling inside. Cheerfulness has an impact on everyone involved.

AN ATTITUDE OF DEPENDENCE ON LEADERSHIP

When you are totally committed to the idea of "my *Lord* working in my life through my *lord*"—your husband gets the message from your attitude. When you trust God to work through your husband, that belief alone sends a message of confidence, esteem, and anxiety-free gentleness. Lean strongly on his leadership in making decisions. The Lord will give you guidance through him, even if he is not a Christian.

"The king's heart is in the hand of the Lord as are the watercourses; He turns it whichever way He will" (Proverbs 21:1). I remember an incident that demonstrates how the Lord can direct. A young lady who was a patient from the local hospital was living with us. She had many problems and her psychiatrist would allow her to be released only to a family. The psychiatrist appeared to be an atheist. I drove her to his office for appointments, and one day he asked me to accompany them into his inner office. "You be in church next Sunday. You need those people," he said to the girl in my presence. A man who did not profess to be a Christian was telling a patient to attend church? At the time, the doctor was her only earthly authority. Yes, I think his heart was in God's hands to turn it for the benefit of the young lady, just as the hearts of our husbands are in His hands.

When we first moved to Atlanta, I had a serious automobile accident in which I suffered a terrible blow on the mouth. I had extensive dental work done—a long, painful process. After some time it became evident the work was inferior. The color of my teeth changed, the root canals failed, and crowns loosened. The dentist who had done the work showed no interest. I began to fret and worry, fearful I would lose my teeth, and it seemed no one cared.

One Sunday morning in desperation I cornered our pastor before the worship service. I told him I was in need of someone to pray with me about my problem and specifically requested that he ask the Lord to answer through Wes. I really wanted Wes to tell me what to do. The pastor agreed and I left for the morning worship service.

Wes wrote a note to me during the sermon. I was surprised because he did not ordinarily do this. It read, "In the morning, call the Emory Dental School." I knew nothing about the school, but I made the call. "I don't know exactly why I am calling, but my husband told me to," I said. I wasn't aware Emory had a program in which dental students care for patients as part of their training. "Oh, you want to be screened," the receptionist said. She set up the appropriate appointments.

My case was such a challenge that I couldn't simply enter the program. The work was too extensive and required expert attention. I left downhearted, but the Lord had something else in mind. I received a call shortly. A special grant was coming in that would provide money for two graduates to do specialty work. They were looking for a challenge. As you might guess, I was selected to be one of their projects.

In the weeks ahead I was given many opportunities to share how the Lord led me to the dental school. A crew of students and department heads often gathered around to inquire how I happened to end up there. "Are you sure you want to know?" I asked, then told my story.

"Dr. Braverman, are you a Christian?" I asked without much thought when I met the young dentist assigned to do my work. You may have guessed that Dr. Braverman was Jewish. It hadn't occurred to me the Lord would give me a Jewish dentist to repair my teeth.

"Well, that's okay," I responded when he replied negatively. "I just thought you should know the Lord has chosen you to do this work, and I know it is going to be an exceptional job." We became great friends over the next year.

An added benefit that pleased Wes and me was having the work done at minimal expense. The school charged primarily for the materials used. In spite of the months of pain, I often had a big smile on my face that Dr. Braverman couldn't understand. It was a great comfort to know I was exactly where God wanted me to be. He had sent me to Emory through the direction of my husband. I knew and understood more than ever how God leads a woman through her husband.

I need reminders of that principle. Some time ago I was about to drive from Atlanta to Columbus, Mississippi to visit our son's family. Two nights before I was to leave, Wes said my car must go to the garage for an oil change. Well, to say the least, it was an irritation.

"You're a fanatic about these cars," I said. He agreed that might be true. I tried to persuade him to allow me to delay because of all I needed to do. But no, the car must go in.

Grudgingly, I went along with the plan. When the mechanic came out to receive the car, I said, "Larry, you and Wes are just fanatics about these cars."

"Yes, but we just want to take real good care of you, Mrs. Cantrell," he replied quietly. He made me ashamed of my attitude but I was far from feeling fully cooperative. In the evening when Wes and I went to pick up the car, there was a note on the seat. "While I had your car in for service I discovered the left rear tire had a spike in it. I have traded it with your spare, but you must have attention given to the tires right away." Most likely I was saved from a serious accident on my five-hour trip.

What a reminder to me to live what I believe. God always works through my husband on my behalf. He does it for us all, whether a husband is lost, saved; mean, nice; drunk, sober; foul-mouthed or well-spoken. God hasn't made a mistake in giving you this man. My *Lord* working in my life through my *lord*! Your *Lord* working in your life through your *lord*!

THE IMPORTANCE OF ATTITUDE

Your attitude can be a pivotal point for your husband. It can pick him up when he's headed down, turn mediocrity into exceptional effort, apathy into interest, plain food into gourmet. Your outlook can carry a man on the brink of good performance into the arena of greatness!

Isn't it a relief to know an attitude is not simply a suggestion, but a **choice** Christians can make because God has equipped us to do so? Ignoring the Scriptures sends your husband into his vocational world unarmed in a way only you *should* arm him.

YOU CAN CHOOSE THE RIGHT ATTITUDE

Train yourself to *choose* a right attitude. When you see it as an act of your will, you don't have to depend on your emotions to dictate your behavior. If you want to evaluate your attitude, simply take note of your reactions. Inappropriate reactions reveal negative attitudes.

You can *choose* the proper attitude. "Let this same attitude *and* purpose *and* [humble] mind be in you which was in Christ Jesus" (Philippians 2:5b). "Fix your minds on them" (Philippians 4:8).

Think about the time when you were first in love and all the nice feelings you experienced. Do you realize the feelings you had *then* are the same ones that would help you be a Godly wife *now*? It was so easy to do right and even to feel the emotion necessary for fulfilling the Scriptural exhortations. Yet those directives are to a wife, not a girlfriend. Why can't you do it now?

The wonderful good news is that you can *choose* to project all the attitudes we've been talking about. You can do everything you felt like doing when you were first in love. Now, you are even better equipped; you know the Lord more closely than ever before. You know your husband much better. You can react differently, not because of how your husband behaves, not based on his merit but because God said so and fully empowers you to do so.

"When they observe the pure *and* modest way in which you conduct yourselves, together with your reverence [for your husband. That is, you are to feel for him all that reverence includes]—to respect, defer to, revere him; [revere means] to honor, esteem (appreciate, prize), and [in the human sense] adore him; [and adore means] to admire, praise, be devoted to, deeply love and enjoy [your husband]" (I Peter 3:2). "Defer to" means choosing to do what he would like. It means not wearing purple if he doesn't like that color. If he prefers long hair, try to have longer hair and wear it in the most becoming way you can. Remember how you deferred to him when you dated? The whole verse sounds like a woman in love, like what you thought you felt when you first grew to love him.

"For it was thus that the pious women of old who hoped in God were (accustomed) to beautify themselves, and were submissive to their husbands—adapting themselves to them as themselves secondary and dependent upon them" (I Peter 3:5). You are not secondary or dependent, but you can *choose* to be submissive and adapt.

"It was thus that Sarah obeyed Abraham (following his guidance and acknowledging his headship over her by) calling him lord—master, leader, authority. And you are now her true daughters if you do right and let nothing terrify you—not giving way to hysterical fears or letting anxieties unnerve you" (I Peter 3:6). "And let the wife see that she respects *and* reverences her husband—that she notices him, regards him, honors him, prefers him, venerates and esteems him; and that she defers to him, praises him, and loves and admires him exceedingly" (Ephesians 6:33b). When you project to your husband the attitudes described in these Scriptures, he feels adored, admired, and significant. We want security; men want to feel significant, or so I've been told many times. We are different not only physically, but also in our thinking, our method of communication, and our feelings.

Now would be a good time to consider where you stand. Any time God confronts us with a new insight or a truth we have already heard, we need to look within ourselves and evaluate. If you confess that your attitudes have not been what you know they should be, you can commit to making the right choices from now on.

Choices! Choices lead to proper attitudes. Jesus made choices (Philippians 2:6-8), and they were always the right ones. He lives in us, and we are enabled to make the right choices that will lead to heart peace. Proper attitudes expressed toward your husband will be his hidden motivator.

7

Get it in Order

Do outside things and people determine what happens to your days? Would you like your life to be more organized and under control? "But all things should be done with regard to decency *and* propriety *and* in an orderly fashion" (I Corinthians 14:40).

I have always known that my husband prefers me to keep everything around us orderly. If I could stay organized, life would be easier for all of us. I am sure that's what you would prefer as well. The first step is to set correct priorities, but if we expect them to be effective in our lives, we must be teachable in spiritual things. It has been a constant learning experience for me.

Three prerequisites for being a teachable person are being in right standing with God, with others, and with ourselves. The Lord has been faithful in making me teachable. He will do the same for you.

First, you must be in right standing with God by having a personal relationship with the Lord Jesus Christ (Romans 10:9, 10; Ephesians 2:8-9; I John 1:9; John 3:3; Matthew 22:37). We must also maintain our fellowship with the Lord by practicing forgiveness. We don't need to beg or plead. We were forgiven **all** on the cross. We need to agree with God at the first quiet prompting of the Holy Spirit that something is wrong. I want to learn to be a "feather duster" Christian—the softest whisper of the Spirit is all I should need to listen, to do, and to correct. I want to avoid being a person who can only be moved by the application of a hammer (reproof) or being hit by a Mac Truck (chastisement) when He has to run over me to make His way known. I'm afraid I must confess that I have often been in the Mac Truck mode.

Don't make a habit of going to bed at night and quickly saying, "Lord, forgive me for *all* my sins." The Lord does not convict people of *sins in general*. The Holy Spirit convicts us of *specific sin*. Satan would like us to feel cleansed by a general confession, but the Lord works with us one small step at a time; one sin at a time.

"Father, forgive me when I am unkind and unforgiving to others" is a general prayer. "Yes, Father, You are right. I was very mean to Sally today, getting even for the remarks she made last night. Thank You for Your forgiveness and enabling me to forgive her. I will ask Sally to forgive me." This is the specific kind of prayer to use as He makes you aware of a particular sin.

The second prerequisite to being teachable is to be in right standing with all people, including brothers and sisters, mothers and dads, children, associates, and acquaintances. That means be able to look anyone in the eye and know in your heart you have done everything possible to make things right according to the Word of God (Matthew 5:23-24). The Lord is interested in our relationships with others, not in our offerings. Take care of the hurt feelings, and then return and make your offering. Many Scriptures deal with relationships and describe how we are to treat others (Matthew 5:22-24; 18:5,15. 21-22; 22:39; Mark 11:25; Ephesians 4:32; Luke 17:4; I Corinthians 16:7; Galatians 6:9; Proverbs 20:22; Colossians 3:13). Other people have never been as much of a problem for me as Wes has. I could almost always justify my anger, unforgiveness, and not asking his forgiveness when I was wrong. The world may never know how ornery we are, but husbands do. The children ultimately will know, but most of all, the Lord *always* knows.

Now I make it a practice to ask Wes's forgiveness as soon as I can come to grips with my inner struggle—anger, frustration, impatience, sharp words, or a bad attitude. I confess it to my *Lord* and my *lord*. It never ceases to amaze me how suddenly *unimportant* the issue I had trouble with seems after I take responsibility for my actions and attitude.

The third prerequisite concerns receiving yourself just as God made you, as we have already discussed. When you are no longer at odds with God, others, and yourself, you are ready to learn. Certainly the Lord has much in store for you, just as I know He does for me.

If you don't settle these prerequisites within yourself, you'll have difficulty receiving any new thoughts and insights the Lord brings you. If you are constantly struggling with your relationship with the Lord, relationships with others, and right thinking about yourself, you can readily see that God cannot take you into a deeper fellowship with Himself. Without a teachable spirit, how can you possibly be the kind of woman God wants you to be for the man to whom you are married? You are not free but in bondage. God says, "And you will know the Truth and the Truth will set you free" (John 8:32). I have begun to walk in new freedom. Won't you join me?

It's comforting to have an orderly list of priorities to refer to and lean on. I've discovered when things go askew and my schedule is hectic, my priorities are usually out of order. I think about my foundational list and ask, what must I do or not do to straighten them out?

There are many things to consider as you make your own list. Do you work outside the home? Does your husband travel a great deal? What ages are your children? Does your husband need more of your time? Do you do all your own housework and home projects?

PRIORITY ONE

My relationship with the Lord and fellowship with Him. "But seek for (aim at and strive after) first of all His kingdom, and His righteousness [His way of doing and being right], and then all these things taken together will be given you besides" (Matthew 6:33). Then everything else that can encumber us will be met without undue concern. "Charm *and* grace are deceptive, and beauty is vain [because it is not lasting], but a woman who reverently *and* worshipfully fears the Lord, she shall be praised" (Proverbs 31:30).

Sometimes church is not a priority. Sometimes reading Scripture is not a priority. I have an acquaintance who demonstrated the latter one night. She is a completed Jew. Even though divorced, she was praying for her husband's salvation and their remarriage. He attended their daughter's basketball game. I couldn't believe my eyes when I looked up in the balcony and saw them seated together. She had a family-sized Bible spread open on her lap facing her ex-husband and she was reading Scripture to him. Even important habits are occasionally inappropriate!

PRIORITY TWO

My husband. I am made to be a "helpmeet, suitable, adapted, and completing;" therefore, he must be a top priority in my life. He is my first ministry. I chose this priority the day I said "I do" and made an oath to God to put Wes first.

There have been many times when my priorities were out of order, but I remember a particular one so well because of the swiftness with which the Lord revealed it to me. I had just purchased a new dress and was very pleased at having a chance to wear it to a meeting where a family friend would preach. Wes came in late and his dinner was waiting. I was not more than a block from the house, when the Lord quietly spoke to my spirit asking, Are your priorities in order?

But Lord, I've done my duty and now I want to enjoy my new dress. I want to hear some good preaching. . . .

Are your priorities in order? He repeated. I turned the car around and headed home knowing I would be greeted by a pleased smile on Wes's face. Inside I was content to have responded correctly **this** time. It's not always something big and obvious that distracts us from the important issues.

PRIORITY THREE

Home and family. Children and housework should never take priority over my husband, nor must housework come before spending time with my children. Even more important is the attitude I communicate to my family about where they stand in my priorities.

Our own children are grown and married now and have increased in number by the addition of four spouses and many grandchildren. They **all** hold high priority. Although they live elsewhere, our home is still important to them and to us. It remains my responsibility to keep it a haven for my husband and a happy place for them to come and visit.

PRIORITY FOUR

Outside ministry. I shouldn't have an outside ministry unless my first three priorities are in order. "She considers a *new* field before she buys *or* accepts it—expanding prudently [and not courting neglect of her present duties by assuming others]. With her savings [of time and strength] she plants fruitful vines in her vineyard" (Proverbs 31:16).

An outside ministry might include a career, teaching a Bible class, or volunteer work. Sometimes we get involved in activities because we mistake the pleading of others for a call from the Lord. We must guard against saying yes to "no" questions. We can't accept new jobs to the neglect of present responsibilities. Make sure the Lord is the one who calls you to a ministry. He won't do so without enabling you, and there will be adequate time to honor your primary commitments.

Number one priority is number one for all eternity. Number two will remain until my husband or I die. I adjust my other priorities to suit our present lifestyle. Number three is still there, though different in nature. You should modify any category following number one according to your circumstances.

Putting the Lord ahead of all else does not mean seek ye the church first. Fellowship with other Christians is very important, but remember your first priority is not a denomination, but our Savior. I am a born-again, blood-washed believer who happens to be affiliated with a particular church. Husbands are won by a wife's godly behavior, not by her church attendance (I Peter 3:1).

A wife may feel uncertain about giving her husband such a high priority. She may not be happy or able to accept the way her marriage is going. Many overlook the flip side of the marriage vows—for richer, for poorer; for better, for worse; in sickness and in health. The romantic young bride may only hear richer, better, and in health. How often the flip side becomes reality! No matter what happens, consult the Word of God in setting your priorities. No matter how undeserving your husband might seem, make him number two.

As you have read the last two chapters, you may have experienced an emotional or spiritual warmth. Perhaps you have even whispered, "Yes, that is what I want in my life." A man made a remark once which has stayed in my memory. When we think about something and experience an emotional warmth, we have a tendency to think we did what we thought simply because we thought about it. So beware of only feeling and thinking about spiritual commitments. You need to **act** upon any commitment which you might feel impressed to make.

If you haven't yet addressed your responsibilities as a wife and made a commitment to the Lord about it, there is no more appropriate time than right now. You need to begin with a commitment to become the kind of woman and wife the Lord wants you to be, especially if you want to be married to a **husband who is known in the gates**. It is a matter of choice.

Once you have done that, addressed the need for a firm foundation in your relationship to the Lord, and set a definitive list of priorities, you are prepared to meet the challenge of a decent and in order life.

8
The "S" Word!

I cannot be submissive on the outside until I am submissive on the inside. This is an old yet a very fresh struggle for me. As I once told Wes, "It's a cinch to live a Spirit-filled life as long as no one crosses me." By the same token, it's easy to be a submissive wife until he asks me to do something with which I don't agree. Just an action won't do the job. Submission is a choice from the heart.

A woman may be weak, but that doesn't mean she's meek or submissive. Children are an excellent example. One who is quiet and seems compliant may turn out to be the more rebellious child in a family. In reality he may be thinking, wait until I get away from here. Submissive behavior without correct heart attitude is not submission.

Some women are naturally *strong* women. They have an opinion about most things. Perhaps they have outstanding leadership qualities. The comments some people, especially men, make about strong women have often annoyed me. After I did an extensive study on the word *strong*, I concluded that it's important to be strong—but about the **right** things.

I'm convinced it takes strength to be a submissive wife, to make a right choice, and to have a right attitude. It takes strength in the Lord. "Not by might, nor by power, but by My Spirit [of Whom the oil is a symbol], says the Lord of hosts" (Zechariah 4:6b). "In conclusion, be strong in the Lord—be empowered through your union with Him; draw your strength from Him—that strength which His [boundless] might provides" (Ephesians 6:10).

The subject of submission brings up discussion, argument and debate, both in churches and out in the world. Women in particular become defensive when the word is even mentioned. We must realize that submission is not a reflection on capability, skill, intelligence, superiority, or strength!

God has created a decent and orderly structure for everything. You would be perplexed to visit Wes's office, ask to see the president, and be referred to six different people who give you six different answers. You'd think, That company is confused; they will never achieve anything worthwhile. They don't have direction. The world is looking at families today and asking much the same thing—who is the head of the home?

God knows and understands us. He is the Creator and Designer. We can perform from the highest level of originality if we do so within His rules of design. We have the most energy and enthusiasm when we live our lives according to His plan.

Women often misunderstand the Scriptures. They read Paul's books to mean woman is inferior. They believe the Word says a woman is less intelligent and less capable than a man. Who is telling these lies? Satan, the accuser, has women bound up in a distortion of truth and is pleased, I am sure, to see them confused. He wants to keep a wife from her Godly design. Then, she will not be content with what God created her to be.

I had to settle, once and for all, what I believed about my role as a wife. If a woman's thinking is confused, her actions will be confused as well. I have been told that in the circus a baby elephant is chained to a stake very early. He soon learns that he can't move far. Even when he is grown and strong enough to break the chain easily, he remains attached. He is free to go, but because he believes he cannot, he does not, held captive by what he thinks. Wrong thinking leads to living out what is not actually true.

Has that happened to you? Check your thinking constantly against the Word. We must think God's thoughts to live out God's ways. Once you have your thinking corrected by God's Word, you can fulfill your role more readily and willingly.

Be reminded, "there is [now no distinction], neither Jew nor Greek, there is neither slave nor free, there is not male and female; for you are all one in Christ Jesus" (Galatians 3:28). If you know that and believe it, you already know you have a unique position with God that is never threatened. Looking at your role as a wife or as a woman in the church, you will see there is no reason to feel threatened. The Scripture makes clear your worth as an individual. You don't need to justify yourself with what some people call Paul's chauvinism. He was simply describing roles. The Scripture does not say woman is weaker but that the man is to treat her *as though* she is (I Peter 3:7).

Honoring a woman as physically the weaker, as Peter says, sounds like a plus to me. Personally, I love the thought.

I often study couples when I attend a function or watch them on the streets and in hotel lobbies. I can always tell a lot about a foolish man's attitude toward women—he walks several steps in front of his wife. We should, however, give our men time to be gentlemen and allow them to treat us as weaker vessels. I think it is great! So don't hurry when getting out of a car; slow down when you approach a door. I enjoy having Wes open doors for me, loosen jar lids, or move heavy furniture.

I am strong, healthy, and agile. For years I was quick to jump out of the car.

"Bernie, would you please sit in the car until I can get around to open your door? If I get out and go in a restaurant or the house and leave you, just sit there until I get back," Wes said to me several years ago. Sometimes I feel strange sitting there waiting for him to get around the car, so I pretend to do something—collect my possessions or check my hair in the mirror.

Let your husband be your protector. Take a deep breath and wait patiently until you've given him the opportunity. Opening doors and walking beside you are small things; however, they are certainly a good beginning.

We often choose the wrong moment to present ideas to our husbands. We tolerate or cope, then have an angry outburst or a pouting period. If your husband waits to tell you something when he is angry, are you teachable and receptive to his request? Share when the situation is pleasant, maybe during one of his favorite meals.

You may be strong, highly motivated, and intelligent, but you can choose to yield humbly in wise obedience to God's designated and divinely appointed authority in your life—your husband. Submission is an attitude, not an act. It is a decision, not an emotion. If you wait until you *feel* submissive, you may never become submissive. It doesn't mean being a doormat. It is insight into the man God has given you—his needs and desires—and choosing to act in accordance with them without his demanding or commanding it.

When you choose to be submissive, emotions will usually fall in line. Other times, they won't cooperate. As we have established, emotions are very unreliable, and you must never allow them to rule your actions.

When David spoke to his emotions, he said that his spirit would rule, not his emotions. "Why are you cast down, O my inner self? And why should you moan over me *and* be disquieted within me? Hope you in God *and* wait expectantly for Him, for I shall yet praise Him, my help and my God" (Psalms 42:5). We should approach negative feelings this way. Satan would like us to be dragged down by our emotions. We will never experience victory if we don't take charge of them.

Are you *secretly* a submissive wife? There are three important reasons for letting your submissiveness show. First, it is a witness to the world. Second, it says whatever my strengths, I can choose to be submissive to God's divinely appointed authority. Third, it can and will have an influence upon others, especially your husband. He'll feel good about himself and about you.

Wes has one story he enjoys telling as an illustration of making a wrong decision because he wouldn't listen to my caution. We were purchasing an automobile and needed a station wagon because of the size of our family. We had only begun to learn about looking to the Lord for all our decisions. This was our first big financial step since making that commitment. We talked to the Lord about a station wagon we had found and agreed that if we could purchase it for a certain amount, it would be His choice. It was a powerful vehicle and happened to be in Wes's favorite color, green. We made our deal and returned later to pick up the wagon and give the salesman a check. He then told us he had made a mistake of $51.00.

"Okay, that's not anything," said Wes.

"But Wes, that's not what we agreed," I spoke up. I don't remember his being rude about it, but he was very firm.

"It's not anything to the Lord. He doesn't care about $51.00; that's close enough," he told me.

"It was the only demon-possessed automobile I ever saw!" Wes comments as he thinks back on the record of that wagon. During the following years we had endless problems with the vehicle. I didn't harp on the matter or remind him of the misjudgement he made. The Lord was doing a good job of that. My part had been to make my appeal at the appropriate time, to allow my husband the freedom to decide, and be cooperative in his decision. The most difficult part is to keep a submissive attitude when we see our husbands making wrong choices, especially when they ignore our opinion or appeal. It's perhaps the most important time to make the choice to speak and then be silent!

Have you determined where you are in your attitude about being submissive? The right moment to make a commitment is now. Correct your thinking and redirect your actions. Ask the Lord to show you the truth, not only in what He says about submission, but also to search your heart and show you about yourself. Do I believe this is true? Do I desire to fit in willingly with God's role for a wife?

Maybe you believe your husband doesn't deserve your submission. Perhaps you are right. After all, who does? Regardless of a husband's condition—deserving or not, Christian or not, Scripture does not offer the option of an unsubmissive attitude. A wife is to be submissive because of his position as her husband.

We need to realize what that means to a husband. He is intended to be the leader in his home. If he is not acting that way, he knows it and his cohorts notice as well. His ego deflates and he may react with rudeness, quiet hostility, or in other ways which won't please you. A husband struggling with headship in his home will find it difficult to take a leadership role at work. Don't let your attitude toward submission hinder your husband. Correcting your thinking is the first step toward victory for you both. Free your husband to be the leader God intends him to be by becoming the submissive wife God intends for you to be.

*Welcome and receive (to your hearts) one another,
then, even as Christ has welcomed and received you,
for the glory of God.*

—Romans 15:7

9

Give Him Freedom

$\mathcal{A}$ woman may marry a man with a "husband improvement program" in the back of her mind or make changing her husband a priority. She can love him to death **but** find an area or two she would like to see changed. Maybe there are several where she feels his mother failed to complete his training. She would like to make up for lost time and improve her man. To anyone so tempted, I say stop feeling responsible for correcting and changing your husband.

Have you ever been in a rainstorm and realized your umbrella had a hole in it? Can you visualize yourself standing in a downpour, trying to fix it? How successful would you be? Trying to change a man is exactly like attempting to patch an umbrella from the underside. You won't succeed. Patch jobs need to come from the "Top side."

One of the greatest contributions you can make to your husband's success is to receive him exactly as he is. "Welcome *and* receive (to your hearts) one another, then, even as Christ has welcomed *and* received you, for the glory of God" (Romans 15:7). How did the Lord receive you? Just as you were.

It is impossible to change anyone through your own efforts, so don't keep any hopes tucked away of doing so. Only the Holy Spirit can bring about change, and He does it from within.

Remember, a successful man is engaged in work that gives him satisfaction and a sense of significance, maintains a good name and reputation, has a rich personal relationship with his wife and family, and is habitually all-out for God. Your part is to be the kind of wife God designed you to be which frees your husband to be a success. In our efforts to change our husbands, we stand in the way of the Lord's work.

Peter speaks of a man's prayers being hindered if his relationship is not right with his wife (I Peter 3:7). I don't suggest you write this Scripture in large letters and put it in his office, but I would make this suggestion: at some moment of sharing you can mention the thought to him. You don't want his prayers hindered, do you? He's likely to pray for you and your family occasionally. Or maybe he doesn't pray at all, but all men come to a point of prayer, even the most agnostic or rebellious. It may be at a time of tragedy, but it will come. Encourage him so he'll be ready when he comes to *his* point of prayer.

You may struggle with the fact that at the end of the day your husband sits down to relax, but you must continue with the same kind of work you've been doing all day. If you happen to have a husband who pitches in, wonderful, but don't try to **make** a man who is not a natural helper into one who is. It won't work.

Think about your girlfriends who don't help. They might sit in the kitchen and talk to you while you are busy, but never offer to aid you in any way. People are different in personality, temperament, gifts, and background. The rest the Lord refines or changes, but only He can do that. The Lord may transform a non-helper into a helper, **but** don't count on it. Remember your commitment to accept your husband as he is.

Not helping doesn't mean he is unloving. Maybe he'll respond if you express how much his lending a hand would mean to you. Perhaps he hasn't understood your need for his assistance. Who knows, he may even enjoy helping. Don't, however, make the mistake of expecting him to change. Be grateful for what he does and never take it for granted.

As I look back over the years, I know I was as proud as could be of the twenty-two year old service technician whom I married. I thought he was the most wonderful man in the world. I had no idea I was marrying a future president/CEO of an international business systems company. You cannot know what is in the future for the man you marry. The leaders, presidents, and billionaires of tomorrow are all unknown; some even seem unpromising as young men. Only God knows His plan for each person. He can explode the potential of an obscure young man and change his direction in an instant.

Are you ready for that? I don't know where your husband is nor what his dreams are. He may be content to do exactly what he is doing right now for the rest of his life. If so, good. If he is not, help him find whatever it is he wants to do. If you haven't accepted him where he is right now, you aren't going to go anywhere else successfully.

If you haven't received your husband as a gift from God, with his potential and limitations, take a few moments right now to do so. Until you settle your reception of him, you won't grow into a better relationship. Reflect upon any thoughts, actions, and attitudes that may have sent him a negative reception message. Confess to the Father about your past struggles and commit to a new beginning. It will free your husband from the feeling of your disapproval. Confess to the Lord those qualities about him which you have been unable to accept. Maybe he drinks, is abusive, lost, profane, has strange quirks, or is basically annoying. Receive him as he is right now, exactly what you need in your life.

"Thank [God] in everything—no matter what the circumstances may be, be thankful and give thanks; for this is the will of God for you . . ." (I Thessalonians 5:18). Give thanks for being married to an old grouch, someone who will never clean the yard, or someone who throws his underwear on the floor. I don't know what your concerns may be, but some wives have unusual concerns.

I had a friend whose husband came in the front door each evening, undressing. His belt went one way; his pants ended up over a door. You could follow his trail as he went through the house. He had other wonderful qualities, but this one was difficult for my friend to accept. Maybe your husband has a similar habit that is difficult to tolerate, much less give thanks for—but it goes with him. Receive and give thanks for **all,** and see if the Lord can't do a better job taking care of it than you can.

Give thanks to the Father for both the potential and the problems that lie ahead, acknowledging the Lord's full control (Romans 8:28). Accepting your husband frees him **and you** from trying to make him over. Sometimes, wives believe they can do a better job of changing their husbands than the Lord can. That is one of the devil's lies. You **can** be a part of it. Free him through acceptance and pray for him when you see an area of need.

If your husband is lost, pray. If he says he is born again and you don't believe he is, speak to him as though he is saved and pray for him as though he is not. Talk to him as though he is saved and treat him that way. A wife's actions, tone of voice, and attitude can be interpreted as accusation and superiority. Love your husband to the Lord with private prayer and godly behavior. You'll be a contented person who can relax with him much more easily, releasing the tension of anxiety, restlessness, or an antagonistic spirit (Philippians 4). It is one of the steps toward the inward peace which comes from obeying the Lord and accepting His design for your life. Give your husband that one *sure* place of acceptance. When the world rejects him, he can face each reproof or challenge more confidently knowing he is secure with his wife. Accepting him frees both of you!

She will comfort, encourage and do him only good as long as there is life within her.

—Proverbs 31:12

10
The President of His Fan Club

$\mathcal{M}$en love admiration. It's not always the most beautiful woman who attracts a man or gets his attention. A somewhat unattractive woman can cultivate manners to attract him through admiration and attentiveness to his individuality. Your husband is very vulnerable to esteem from others if you fail to give it to him.

One night when Wes arrived home, he said, "Bernie, a lady at the office told me today that I was the most thoughtful husband she had ever known." My ears pricked up. If a woman of questionable character had complimented my husband, he probably wouldn't have paid as much attention. Listen to the remarks other women make to your husband. What he repeats to you or to others could expose his greatest area of need.

What about your husband? Does he often ask you about his appearance? After you thank him for a gift, does he continue to ask,

"Are you sure you like it?" I hope you repeat compliments and expressions of love and gratitude to him. Once is not enough. You never tire of hearing him say how much he loves you or how great he thinks you look, do you?

I realized Wes needed more attention for his thoughtfulness. Maybe I hadn't been complimenting him often enough? We seem to be more sensitive when openly attentive females are around, but that may not be the greatest danger. Their less obvious approach may be more cause for concern. Part of your responsibility is to meet your husband's need for admiration so such encounters won't be a temptation to him. If you are married to a nice fellow, he probably has many fans, a lot of them women. You'd be wise to be the president of his fan club. **Encouragement** is the key to holding that position.

We were attending a board meeting at a very nice resort. They were honoring Wes for his thirty-five years with the company. The chairman said some nice things about him and his time with Lanier. Since Wes would be honored again later, they wanted to recognize me by presenting a beautiful piece of Waterford crystal. Wes and I were delighted. As we were being seated, the chairman asked, "Bernie, is there anything you would like to say?" Much to his surprise, I answered, "Well, as a matter of fact, there is!" I took the mike and made a brief but glowing speech about Wes. I paid tribute to his loyalty and faithfulness, not only to Lanier, but to me.

Always be ready to build up your husband, especially to his men friends and business associates. Welcome every opportunity to speak on his behalf. If you are thinking the right thoughts, you'll be ready to do it anytime.

Encouragement comes in many forms. I'll give you some hints and suggestions, but you must *know* your man. When you dated, most likely you learned everything you could about him, didn't you? You discovered his favorite colors, styles, and hairdos. If he liked athletic types, you tried new sports. If he enjoyed good cooking, you bought cookbooks and aprons. You were looking for ways to appeal to him. Isn't that true?

Becoming a better wife will be the greatest encouragement to your husband. As you grow into the kind of wife he needs, he may never say a word. It may appear he hardly notices. Be warned—this is a one-way street, no fifty-fifty proposition. We would like it to be 100 percent mutual, but we are only responsible for ourselves. Remember you are the one who is completing, adapting, and suitable. You'll feel as though you are giving 200 percent most of the time. You enter into this commitment with no strings attached—except to achieve the heart peace that comes from obedience to the Lord.

One special gift you can give your husband is your prayer support. "The earnest (heartfelt, continued) prayer of a righteous man makes tremendous power available—dynamic in its working" (James 5:16b). That means us, too. I hope your relationship will grow to the point where you'll be sharing your most intimate needs, and he will share with you the everyday trials, stresses, and decisions he faces, asking you to pray with him about them. If not, pray for him in secret. As the opportunities come, you can let him know that you pray for him daily and even express specifics about your requests or thanksgivings.

A good fan is always loyal. Loyalty is a treasured quality. It should go beyond the husband-wife relationship and be a part of all our relationships. "He who goes about as a talebearer reveals secrets; therefore associate not with him who talks too freely" (Proverbs 20:19). If you are disloyal to others, your husband may think you would be disloyal to him as well.

Sharing builds understanding. Timing is a key to encouraging him to share. Don't wait until tense moments arrive and then say accusingly, "You never tell me anything. I'm always left in the dark." Talk when circumstances are pleasant. It may be very difficult for you both, but it will be worth the effort.

All of us like to feel cherished, and little things are a great help. Be sure you never deliberately embarrass your husband, but tell him privately how you feel if something is bothering you. In one of those sweet times together, simply express how you would appreciate his doing thoughtful deeds for you. Decide on the ones which are most important to you, like taking out the garbage, opening the doors, or calling during the day.

Encourage your husband to dream, to have purpose, and to set goals. Give him a blank book in which to write down his thoughts and hopes, if that's something you think might appeal to him. Let him know you'd love him to talk to you about them. When you understand his innermost thoughts, you can look toward the same objectives. True companionship is not made up of two people gazing at each other by candlelight; it develops when they share a sense of direction and can go forward together.

One day Wes and I were reminiscing about some of our early dreams and how the Lord brought them to fruition.

"Every dream I ever dreamed businesswise has come true," he said. Most of it took time, a lot of time! Very little came true quickly.

At a leadership conference Wes attended, they were to write down a dream inventory. The leader asked them to include anything they had thought about, even if it seemed absurd. About six months later, Wes happened to glance through his list, which he had since forgotten. Everything had come true. Does that mean Wes sat around and fantasized about ridiculous accomplishments? Certainly not.

"Delight yourself also in the Lord, and He will give you the desires *and* secret petitions of your heart. Commit your way to the Lord—roll and repose [each care of] your load on Him; trust (lean on, rely on and be confident) also in Him, and He will bring it to pass" (Psalms 37:4-5). When Wes was remembering fulfilled dreams, he added the comment, "My only explanation is that the Lord let me in on His plans." He perceived God's desires as his own. The Lord will cause you to desire His desires. Your responsibility is to delight in Him, then you can trust that your desires are correct and His guidance.

Two dream fulfillments that we experienced personally stand out in my mind. Wes and I spent a very short time on the Gulf coast for our honeymoon. Late on that February afternoon we stood on the beach at sunset.

"Wouldn't it be wonderful to live here someday?" I asked him. Neither of us could have manipulated circumstances to make such a move happen, but within seven months, the company transferred him to the area and we lived a short distance from the very spot.

During another summer several years later, we were invited to stay at a house on Lake Lanier near Atlanta. We were living in Baton Rouge and were delighted to spend some time in such a special place.

It was a wonderful week. We enjoyed the beauty of the water and the fantastic location of the house.

"We could never have a lake home," I said one afternoon when we were out on the lake fishing. Wes asked why I would say such a thing.

"After experiencing this beautiful place, I would never want a different one." Within five years the company had transferred us to Atlanta, and we owned and enjoyed that lovely lake house for nine years.

Dreams can come true, if we will only be sensitive to the still small voice inside that clues us in on what God is up to. When they do, don't fail to know and acknowledge the Source. Don't get *elbowitus* from patting yourself on the back. The Lord brings dreams to fruition if we cooperate with Him. He is the true Dream-Fulfiller! "Now to Him Who, by (in consequence of) the [action of His] power that is at work within us, is able to [carry out His purpose and] do superabundantly, far over *and* above all that we dare ask or think—infinitely beyond our highest prayers, desires, thoughts, hopes or dreams" (Ephesians 3:20).

Sell your husband on being enthusiastic. "Whatever may be your task, work at it heartily (from the soul), as [something done] for the Lord and not for men" (Colossians 3:23).

If your husband can see the relationship his particular job has to the entire company, he will automatically become more enthusiastic. He'll see the importance of his contribution to the whole.

You may have heard the story about two bricklayers working on the same project but at opposite ends of the building. A gentleman walking along on the street asked one of them what he was doing. "I am laying brick," he replied. The man walked on around the block and encountered the second bricklayer.

"I am building a cathedral," he answered when asked the same question. Same building, same work, but a different perspective. Which of them do you think would make the more interesting husband?

Wes and Wesley, our son, were installing a new water heater at our house. They completed the installation, but there was one other nasty task to be done. We lived on a hill, and the old tank had to be taken down to the curb for removal. Every time the two men (one a nine year old) tried to hoist it onto the wheelbarrow, it rolled off. Several attempts later the youngster said, "Dad, why don't we just roll it down the hill?" Wes gave an embarrassed laugh, and they did! He was so close to the problem he missed the obvious. He learned an interesting principle: you can focus on the objective and neglect to use the best method, or you can focus on the best method and do the wrong thing. In either case, you have lost your perspective. You may simply need to expand it. You can help your husband by encouraging him to broaden his perspective about his job.

Perhaps you also need to do that. Reading about his kind of work will increase your understanding and listening carefully to his discussions with others will, too. You need to keep in mind that your objective is to encourage and support but *not* to lead him. The more you understand, the better equipped you are to challenge him to see things enthusiastically.

Help this special person in your life to be a lifelong learner—one way is by being one yourself. Encourage him to read good books, attend seminars, and seek additional schooling, then give him time and space to do them without interruption.

Choosing the wrong kind of friends can affect our husband's enthusiasm. By not being as selective as we should, we fail to choose friends who can influence attitudes for the best. We need to take heed of the Scripture, "He who walks [as a companion] with wise men shall be wise, but he who associates with [self-confident] fools will [be a fool himself and] shall smart for it" (Proverbs 13:20). Enthusiasm is contagious, so you can help your husband by developing friends who are enthusiastic.

Two specific relationships taught me about the influence of friends. There was a woman who was as close to me as a sister, but she became involved in an entirely different way of life. She and her husband were drifting apart, and she was having a ball on her own. Wes and I were struggling in our relationship at the same time. Being so close, she knew it. I thought I could be a good influence on her, but before long I realized I was the one being influenced. I was allowing her independent spirit to stir up a lot of rebellious attitudes in me.

In the other case I was beginning to spend a great deal of time with the wife of a business associate of Wes's. We enjoyed many of the same activities and projects. Even though I never planned it, our conversation frequently drifted to husbands and the company; it always headed downhill and became a gripe session. I was usually left with negative feelings toward both.

There's a little game women play. I'm sure you're familiar with it. I call it "Can you top this?" They get together and match stories about the thoughtless acts their husbands have done. Everyone chimes in with a tale to top the last one. If you get involved in a similar game, take the lead and start with a story of support and encouragement. It will help other wives look at their husbands in a positive manner when you relate pleasant happenings and praise rather than priding yourself on being in the most difficult marriage or having the most to cope with. Don't however go too far the other way and demonstrate pride or make them envy you. You can be proud of good things, or you can take pride in having a difficult life. Either way is wrong.

I heard a preacher friend tell a barnyard story that I think makes the point very well. He likened animals to church members. The buzzard doesn't fly, he floats on air currents and only comes down when he smells a stench. The preacher talked about many other animals, but I especially liked what he said about the sheep which he described as a very dirty animal. If it develops a sore on its body, it looks for another sheep with the same problem. They rub sores to relieve the pain and itching.

Be careful not to seek out people with whom to compare problems, but encourage others to win over difficult circumstances. Determine to have a positive impact on others. When we realize our friends are having a negative influence in our lives, we have to move away from those friendships or else win victory over our thoughts and conversation and become the influencer, not the influenced.

I married an enthusiast. Wes had a way about him, a habit of looking at a problem as an opportunity. The man was so enthusiastic, I believe it even affected his appearance. He has always looked younger than his age, but several years ago, it occurred to me that Wes seemed to have aged a lot in a short period of time. I began to study him more closely. After a few weeks and much thought, I decided to have a talk with him.

"Wes, I have something I need to share with you. (long pause) You are looking old," I said cautiously. With a look of surprise and apprehension, he gave me his immediate and total attention. He wasn't accustomed to the president of his fan club saying anything like that.

"Honey, I noticed it several weeks ago, and I've been trying to figure out why. I think I have the answer," I quickly added. "You've lost the glint in your eye."

"Well, I can do something about that," he said with relief in his voice. And he did! He got the glint back in his eye. That one communication covered a great deal of territory for him. It said, "You have allowed some business associates, something at work, or unfortunate circumstances to pull you down. You're not soaring above them like an eagle like you usually do."

Wes's circumstances did not change immediately, and some relational difficulties remained; but he changed his attitude. He made a choice, a correct one. You should encourage your husband to do likewise. Sometimes things go wrong and feelings hit the pits. That's the time to encourage his enthusiasm even when he doesn't feel that way and nothing seems to warrant it.

Even when you don't *feel* enthusiastic, act that way. You can be excited about life even though it's raining, a tire is flat, the fuel gauge just hit empty, the children are sick, or your husband loses his job; but the Son will still be shining on the inside. You can make the right choice.

Be alert to times your husband is discouraged. Wes has occasionally had "bad ink" in publications. Once when he was concerned over a writer's comments, I wrote out this Scripture for him to put on his desk: "*But* no weapon that is formed against you shall prosper, and every tongue that shall rise against you in judgement you shall show to be in the wrong." (Isaiah 54:17a).

One aspect of being your husband's chief fan is not quite as pleasant. It requires a great deal of love, sensitivity and timing; but you must help keep his feet on the ground so success won't go to his head. "Every one proud *and* arrogant in heart is disgusting, hateful *and* exceedingly offensive to the Lord. Pride goes before destruction, and a haughty spirit before a fall" (Proverbs 16:5, 18). Once I asked Wes, "Honey, how do I help you keep your feet on the ground?"

"That's easy," came his quick answer. We live on a hill with a valley between the house and the street. It is a breathless five-hundred-foot trip to keep the garbage can on wheels from running off on its own, and hard pushing is necessary to get it back up to street level. "I wanted the garbage company to pick it up at the rear of the house," Wes went on, "but you said you thought the regular way would be good exercise for me. It's true, Bernie. When I start out and smell the aroma of that garbage, I think, Well, you're not such a big shot after all."

When two of the little grands were visiting, I collected one of my favorite grandmother stories. Four year old Caleb was a great helper. One afternoon I asked him to help me straighten up the books and magazines I keep stacked near Wes's chair. As we worked together, each lost in our own little area of responsibility, Caleb made a remark.

"Grandmama, this reminds me of Paw-Paw." I turned to see what he was looking at, and sure enough there was Wes featured on the cover of a magazine.

"Caleb," I replied, "that is your Paw-Paw."

"What would he be doing on the front of a magazine?" the little man asked rolling his big brown eyes at me.

"Caleb, your Paw-Paw is a very important man," I said after a moment's thought.

"Paw-Paw is a Paw-Paw, he's not a very important man!" he said with an air of skepticism and strong conviction in his voice.

I could hardly wait to share this incident with Wes when he returned from a trip. I knew he would enjoy the antics of his grandson, the truth of what the little boy said, and another reminder of who he is. He laughed heartily when I told him and was disappointed not to have had the story to use in his speech the night before.

Along career routes, it's easy to lose your focus and begin to think highly of yourself when promotions or rewards or compliments come your way. The Scripture reminds us of the origin of promotion. "For not from the east nor from the west nor from the south come promotion *and* lifting up. But **God is the judge!** He puts down one and lifts up another" (Psalms 75:6,7, emphasis added).

I am very proud of Wes and his accomplishments. I could easily drift into thinking **we** have done great things. That Psalm brings us back to a realistic perspective, recognizing anew Who is in charge.

"Your comments were wonderful. However, I know I must treat them as I would a great perfume. Take a whiff and enjoy the scent, but be careful not to swallow it," I heard a speaker say after being given a marvelous introduction. As your husband does well in his endeavors, the temptation is there to swallow the whole success as a tribute to his own efforts. Help him to keep a healthy perspective on the Source of his success. You do it with quiet reminders, not with negatives. The best results will come from your own gratitude to the Lord and recognition of His blessings through your husband.

Be your husband's greatest admirer. Keep him in mind through the day and ask the Lord to give you creative ideas for expressing your admiration, gratitude, and sincere appreciation. He needs it all. Admiration is the driving force behind a fan.

Would you be comfortable saying sweet remarks and compliments such as these to your husband? I love to hear you laugh; it makes your eyes shine. You tell jokes so well; I wish I could remember them the way you do. You're so disciplined about preparing in advance. How did you develop that habit? I learn something new every time I hear you teach. You are the best . . . (lover, kisser, husband, friend). I can't believe how fortunate I am to have you. You are the most fun to be with. You're my best friend. What would I do without you?

You need to evaluate your role as his fan club president. How do you rate? A great fan not only admires and loves the hero, but is faithful in telling him so. A man "known in the gates" surely should know of his wife's love and admiration.

Let every man be quick to hear, (a ready listener,) slow to speak, slow to take offense and to get angry.

—James 1:19b

11
A Lost Art

*H*ave you been working to earn a good reputation with your husband by developing the lost art of active listening? Does he view you as his chief prayer warrior and feel free to share his burdens with you?

The way you listen will determine how often he confides in you. He will observe how well you listen and watch to see what you do with what he says. If he shares something that happened at the office or how his boss or co-worker mistreated him, beware of taking up the offense for him. You cannot take on responsibility for resolving the problem, so you must win the battle with your emotions and with the desire to get even. Generally, husbands like wives to be concerned, but they don't want them to play a mother role.

I learned a lesson from our son about listening and reacting to what you hear. We didn't have many clothes and we wore what we had, even if we weren't very fond of them. Bell-bottom pants were popular when Wesley was a little boy, and my mother made a navy, red, and white pair for him. He didn't like those pants but didn't say much about it. One day he came in from school and said that when he went into class his teacher had said, "Oh, we have a new little girl in our class today." That afternoon the teacher happened to call me about something else. In a controlled voice, deliberately softened, I told her I was upset about her remark.

"Mrs. Cantrell, I never said any such thing," she said. Our son knew that if he simply protested about the pants, I wouldn't hear his petition. But if his teacher implied he looked like a girl, I'd get rid of the problem; the pants, that is. I had jumped to a conclusion about what I heard without asking meaningful questions.

Of course, the important aspect of the situation was that Wesley got caught in a most creative lie. It convinced him that he could never lie and get away with it. It was a good lesson for both of us. With our husbands, too, we must be careful not to assume we have heard the whole story when we learn only one side. Always listen, be loyal, and don't break his confidences, but don't assume the responsibility or take up the offense.

I wrote a script for an hour-long workshop on the wife's role that I was going to give at a women's conference and asked Wes to critique it for me, red pen in hand. He was to cross out anything that didn't have harmony with his spirit. When I came back Wes was sitting very quietly, and the paper didn't have a mark on it. "Bernie," he asked, "did you write this? It's great. I wouldn't change a word of it—except for one thing. You wrote 'men want active, intelligent listening from their wives, but I am convinced they seldom want advice!' Sweetheart, I don't agree with that statement."

I went off to think about it and came to see that my idea should be somewhat modified. I'm convinced that a wife has to earn the right, privilege, or responsibility of giving him advice. I believe a husband seldom wants it, but *may* occasionally. . . .

When you have observed your husband over a period of time, maybe you'll know if and when he sincerely does want your advice. Be cautious about speaking and do it thoughtfully after seeking God's wisdom. Do not take advantage when your husband reveals his weaknesses or you will quickly lose the privilege. If you do give what you consider to be good, sound advice, don't expect him to follow it. And **please** don't check up to see if he took it. "Anxiety in a man's heart weighs it down, but an encouraging word makes it glad" (Proverbs 12:25). "The mind of the [uncompromisingly] righteous studies how to answer" (Proverbs 15:28a). "He who answers a matter before he hears the facts, it is folly and shame to him" (Proverbs 18:13).

I'm convinced the greatest quality of being a good listener is to be selfless, concentrating on the speaker. You demonstrate that you value your husband by listening carefully to his words and being attentive to his emotions. You'll know what I mean if you remember the times when you had something important to tell your husband. He nodded casually, looked at the television, or let his eyes settle on his newspaper. You felt rejected (not that you were rejected, only that you *felt* that way). You might even have asked, "Are you listening?" Even though he said yes, his body language sent a different message.

When challenged, he could probably recite word for word what you said; he recorded, but did not *hear*.

If we wanted to be recorded, we'd just buy a machine. I desire active participation, don't you? Well, if *you* want obvious interest, what about your husband? He feels exactly the same way. Use body language to express your interest in him and to say he has your undivided attention. Let it express attentiveness and say, You are priority number one, everything else is set aside, and I am listening to you.

My mom is a great listener. Young and old are drawn to her because she listens carefully and hears what they are saying. At our children's parties we often found mom in the middle of a circle listening intently. It gives us a clear message; people need people who will sit down and listen to them.

You'll be a fascinating woman if you learn to listen. Your husband will develop the same good skills by watching you. The best listener is one who knows all about a subject listening closely to a person who knows nothing about it. If you want your husband to be your spiritual leader and teacher, learn to listen. You may rehear what you already know, but treat it as something new. If you aren't attentive, he may hesitate to talk about the very subjects you'd like for him to discuss with you. He wants your support and he needs you to show your interest by asking meaningful questions. There are, however, times to be quiet and simply give him your undivided attention. It could be exactly what he needs to resolve a problem or bolster his morale.

Men and women don't express themselves the same ways even though they use the same language. Understanding what your husband wants to say but doesn't know how is a more difficult and deeper part of listening. I believe God has gifted woman with intuition enabling her to understand—*if she has the desire*, but take care not to overestimate that intuition or trust it too much because it may not always be accurate. He may not be thinking what you think he is thinking!

Years ago Wes was giving his testimony at a church in Douglasville, Georgia. The children and I, along with my mother-in-law who was a member there, were seated near the front. It could have been that I was in a special frame of mind that particular weekend. I may have been thinking what a lucky girl I was to have Wes. Maybe Mr. Wonderful's armor was extra shiny on that special day, I don't know. I learned something very important later in the week when the pastor told Wes's mother, "You can tell that young woman truly loves her husband. Her eyes never left his face the whole time he was speaking." How pleased I was the pastor chose to make the comment to her and that she told me. I automatically registered the importance of watching his face, as I hope you will. I wasn't aware of the message I was sending nor that I was studying my husband so carefully, but I was sure glad I did! Now I do it consciously when he speaks privately and publicly.

Eye contact is an important part of real communication, so pay careful attention to where you focus. With a little effort it can become a lifelong habit that is a great morale builder. The fringe benefit is that you'll be learning more about that special person God has placed in your life.

Because you are your husband's "glory, majesty and preeminence," people look at you to evaluate what kind of man he is

(I Corinthians 11:7b). They judge your feelings about him when they observe how you look at him. Decide now to do this one small but important thing. You may be surprised how it builds a new feeling in you. What an asset to your husband you can be as a good, responsible listener. He'll gain an air of success under your watchful gaze and attentive listening.

How would your husband and family answer if they were asked if you are a good listener? No improvement will come until a woman is honest with herself. If after close scrutiny you can't answer with a positive, it's a good time to start developing this wonderfully attractive skill. If you cultivate active listening, you'll be better prepared to listen to your gentleman while he learns how to listen to you and to others.

12
What About Me?

*W*e have watched many couples among our acquaintances grow apart for various reasons. The primary one, I feel, is that someone wasn't working at growing **together**. God only needs one willing heart to draw a family together and toward Him. I remember the first time I heard a Bible teacher say it. As I left the class I kept thinking, "I can be that one!" If the Spirit of the Lord indwells each spouse, as they grow closer to the Lord they will draw nearer to one another. Every marriage may not be so well established. Even if both of you are growing Christians, you can't be dependent upon your husband's progress alone, maybe it's you who will have to settle contentedly on being the one willing heart.

If you wait until things seem hopeless, it will be much more difficult. Be willing early even when there are no serious problems. God has much in store for a willing heart.

Let personal development make you more of a challenge, a more exciting person. Be a better listener because you are an *educated* listener. Above all, know what it means to walk closely with the Lord, to put your husband first, and to be a good mother.

Growth in your personal fellowship with the Lord is top priority. You certainly will become more beautiful. I love this beauty formula and really count on it for myself. I'm sure you'll want to join me. "And all of us, as with unveiled face, [because we] continued to behold [in the Word of God] as in a mirror the glory of the Lord, are constantly being transfigured into His *very own* image in ever increasing splendor *and* from one degree of glory to another; [for this comes] from the Lord [Who is] the Spirit" (II Corinthians 3:18).

The work *in you* is the Lord's responsibility. "For we are God's [own] handiwork (His workmanship)" (Ephesians 2:10a). "And I am convinced *and* sure of this very thing, that He Who began a good work in you will continue until the day of Jesus Christ" (Philippians 1:6a). *Being available* for His work in you is your responsibility. Be available to be made beautiful by being in fellowship with Him through reading His Word and praying.

As you grow closer to the Lord, you become a spiritual challenge to your husband. He may say to himself, That wife of mine is so much like what I think Jesus is like. She knows how to say the right thing to encourage me toward good. When she's around, I think about Jesus more. When I am around her, I want to be more like Him. What must your husband do to make sure he is leading you? He may see that he needs to get ahead; challenge him to *run* ahead.

God created man with all the raw material to be the leader in his family. I hope you haven't been guilty of saying your husband is not the spiritual leader in your home. He is leading, but he may be going in the wrong direction. If the desire to lead is deeply buried, there may be creative means for you to help him become aware of it by looking to him for leadership, treating him in the ways the Word instructs, and your own personal growth.

When the Lord knows you have a heart for Him, He is going to work in your husband's life more than ever. You must get out of the way. I Peter 3:1-6 paints a beautiful picture of a wife's role in motivating her husband. You can encourage your man to have a relationship with the Lord and a closer walk with Him.

We should always be learning. Many wonderful opportunities are available. No woman has a legitimate excuse for ignorance about any subject. Books, magazines, seminars, Bible studies, church, adult education, community colleges, and other resources are all around us. First, pursue those endeavors that help you to be a better wife.

When we moved to Atlanta, I read an advertisement about a Dorothy Carnegie course. Wes had often recommended Dale Carnegie courses to young sales representatives, and I knew he thought they were very good. I was instantly interested. Wes consented for me to have an interview and was willing to invest in my taking the course.

The class met only one night a week, so it didn't require my being away from the family very much. I made new friends, and discovered more of my capability to interact with others and a talent for public speaking. I believe my desire to take the course pleased Wes, and he enjoyed my returning home enthusiastic and excited over receiving honors. I am not suggesting that everyone take this particular course, but that you should follow your desires to expand your perspective and stimulate growth and improvement.

Be sensitive to the desires the Lord places in your heart. You should do those things which He leads you to do and not imitate someone else. We cannot mimic one another and compare ourselves and hope to please Him. We are so special, unique, different—we must continue in our "own bent," ready and willing to grow in our individual way (Proverbs 22:6).

I have a friend who is a perfect example of a wife who wanted to grow but chose the wrong way. She was caught up in academic life and began to think of achieving more and more in her career. Emotionally, she drifted further and further from home. Finally, she left her husband, children, and home. She grew away from her number two priority.

Several years ago our pastor requested that I take a special counseling course. The church was sponsoring a well-known counselor who flew in from out of state for several weekends to teach. What an opportunity! Wes was happy to finance my venture, especially since the pastor had asked me. Just one more opportunity to learn, to grow, to expand my perspective.

Are you prepared to be a credit to your husband, the kind of woman whom the kind of husband you would like to have married would want to marry? We often contemplate, If only he were . . . when we should be thinking, Maybe he could be . . . if I were. . . . A lot of husbands outgrow their wives through exposure and education. It begins to show in looks, conversation, and attitudes. Don't be stuck in the comfortable mediocrity of existence. Learn what you can, grow where you will, and be what and who God created you to be.

My husband is a constant learner. He has quick comprehension and strong powers of concentration. He reads, studies, and observes. He exposes himself to people from whom he can learn. Maybe your husband is that way, too. If not, encourage him by becoming a consistent learner yourself. Just remember to keep a good, healthy attitude so he'll be approving and challenged without feeling put down or resentful.

I enjoy observing couples but sometimes feel sad about them. Many seem united in growth, but others don't look as if they belong together. The man is well dressed and immaculate in every detail. But his wife, probably walking several steps behind, is inappropriately attired. That can happen simply because she has watched her husband grow without attempting to learn in her own world. With sensitivity to the Spirit and to the many opportunities all around, you can easily overcome any inequalities of growth.

I had a keen interest in interior design. It was a needed skill for me with all the moves and different homes we lived in. I wanted to have confidence in myself about decorating, but most of all, I wanted Wes to have confidence in my ideas. Continuing adult education classes in design were available, and I took advantage of them. After three years, I earned my certificate and obtained my license. The reward, the blessing is being better equipped to help young women, including those in my own family. The greatest benefit is that I have confidence to make our home portray comfort, warmth, and my husband's success.

For several years I belonged to a neighborhood investment group. We did well, but most of all we learned about an area of life we had never experienced. Wes was always interested in knowing what we were doing and what information our decisions were based on. It gave us a whole new realm of shared interest.

I have enjoyed learning, and I pray I will never reach the point of not having a desire to learn. Where are you right now? It's an excellent time to consider areas where you might be able to grow. Write down some of the opportunities of which you could take advantage.

If nothing immediately comes to mind, commit it to the Lord and ask Him to lead you. Every aspect of your life as a born-again is spiritual, so the Lord may lead you to projects which are not church related but are nevertheless His will for your life. Be sensitive to the Spirit. He will show you how to grow and equip you for advancement. We don't want to join the ranks of the *girls who were left behind.*

13
But I Want to Be a Career Woman!

*M*any of my peers are out in the job force now. They've reared their children and have more time to do other things. It seems right for them, but I have deep concern for those who must go to work while they still have young children at home. Their husbands are struggling in the workplace and need support at home.

At the time Wes and I married, I was already working, and we never discussed my not working. We spent our earnings carefully and without much discussion saved a large portion of our small incomes. When he received a promotion seven months later and we moved, we were grateful that we had.

As soon as we were settled in our new location, I began interviewing for another job and had a good offer. Then, we learned I was pregnant. We discussed my working until shortly before the baby's arrival but decided it would be unfair to allow an employer to invest time and money in my training. It was a wise decision.

I was at home to support Wes in his new position and help with the phone and paperwork. His income wasn't much. We learned to be creative with our small savings account as he strove to learn his new work. Without those savings, we would have gone into debt just to live. I never doubted that Wes would make it. Even though I didn't know much about the woman in Proverbs 31, my feeling secure about his ability played an important part in his increasing confidence and success.

Promoting the good health and happiness of a husband or family is a time-consuming responsibility. To have as priority the best interests of the man you love is a most rewarding career for a wife, and for me it has been fulfilling. I don't underrate the women who have been forced by circumstance to take outside jobs. Frankly, I look at many of them and shake my head with wonder and respect at all they seem to accomplish. The job of helping a husband get ahead is such a demanding one that I wonder where the energy comes from that allows a woman to manage her own career and have enough left over to support her husband in his. It must be difficult.

If you work outside the home, be sure it's for the right reasons and not to escape the mundane or to appease a world that implies women who stay at home lack adequate intelligence and abilities. I do realize some must work elsewhere to supplement their husbands's salaries.

If there is any way you can stay at home, do it though it may call for sacrifice! Be creative about doing things in your home rather than paying others to do them. You may even find opportunities to supplement the family income within the home.

With four children, a lovely house, and many responsibilities in taking care of them and being Wes's support team, I can't explain why I suddenly became interested in working outside the home nor why I let it become a driving desire. Perhaps I began to feel a need to get out in the world or wanted to earn some money of my very own! Maybe I heard some of the comments working women make about those who choose to stay home. It's hard to say.

I overheard a friend at church speaking to a lady about employment with him. He was editor of a magazine, something that interested me very much. I began to talk about that job with Wes and with Carl. He wasn't overly enthusiastic about hiring me. It didn't occur to me that his hesitance probably came from the obvious need for me to be at home.

A wonderful woman came to work for me every day. She loved the children, was a great housekeeper, and was willing to be there ten to twelve hours a day for little compensation. She played an important part in my easy decision to go to work for Carl.

I was so excited that I turned a deaf ear to any reservations I felt. Wes was tolerant about my long hours. I had to catch up on my typing skills and wanted to learn everything I could about the magazine business.

In a few weeks the Lord graciously made possible another promotion for Wes, and it meant moving to Atlanta. In that short time I realized how "caught up" I had become in my career. Carl became enthusiastic when he discovered my willingness to work hard and long and that I actually was a capable person. I loved the challenge of moving into new areas of responsibility, like going out on interviews and field trips to gather information for articles. The problem was neither with the job nor with my enthusiasm; it was simply that I had lost sight of my first three priorities.

I must add that during those weeks, my house was in order and the children weren't neglected, but I was exhausted when not pumped up with my hypermetabolism and surging adrenalin. My church work continued, my clothes needed extra attention for the office, and I am sure the children felt a void with my absense. And Wes? Well, I guess I blocked his reactions and comments from my mind. Super mom and super church woman and super wife and super career girl! Just writing about it tires me now. For weeks, I was totally devoted to my new career, yet when Wes told me about his promotion and our pending move, I never looked back with longing or regret. I had learned a valuable lesson.

Temptation is always lurking out there somewhere—a career opportunity, the exciting challenges of different stimuli. Cling to your precious home life as long as you have a choice. You'll be glad you did. It doesn't mean you don't have a wonderful brain if you want to be a career homemaker. I believe it takes a strong woman to say, I am smart. I am bright. I choose to channel my capabilities into my husband's support, our home, and children. You'll be the oddball. Occasionally, you'll be labeled in unattractive terms. Join me in exposing that falsehood. "Her husband boasts of and praises her, saying, many daughters have done virtuously, nobly and well [with the strength of character that is steadfast in goodness] but you excel them all. Her children rise up and call her blessed" (Proverbs 31:28b,29). Your children will call you blessed not because of how you treat them, but for your love of their dad. They will see the order of your priorities and rejoice.

In August 1989, *Fortune* magazine's cover story was entitled "The CEO's Second Wife." I was very disappointed in it. It seemed so unfair to place such emphasis on the 12 percent failure rate of their marriages and ignore the enduring 88 percent. Only a few months later, *Fortune* invited Wes and me to an anniversary dinner party. I sat next to the editor of the magazine. During the evening we discussed the article, and I suggested he do one about the good marriages.

"Now Bernie," he said, "you know it wouldn't sell." I told him that what disturbed me most was making all first wives seem dull, dowdy, and dumpy. After stimulating conversation about this and other interests, the evening came to a close. As we were leaving, he came over to Wes.

"You got a trophy wife the first time!" he said. Of course I was pleased when Wes told me about it later. We receive that kind of approval when we determine to learn and be interesting to everyone we meet.

I'm convinced a marriage has a greater chance of survival as well as truly being an earthly picture of Heaven when a man and wife have mutual interests and goals. Many women do outside work and have a hard time having to do it. God put in us girls a need to feel secure and cherished. If we are out in the marketplace fighting the dragons along with our husbands, no one is waiting at home to comfort the weary. That's a problem.

So often working women have a misconception about what's expected of them. Many believe they must dress in a manly way in order to be taken seriously. Some adopt language they think will allow them to relate to men more readily. Thus they fail to take into the marketplace their uniqueness as women, the feminine traits which are valuable in all areas of life. They become just like any other cat in the jungle of life. Regardless of where we are required to fulfill our responsibilities, we must retain our individuality and the qualities that make us different from men.

Encouraging women to stay at home is not meant to discourage those who are in the work force. My intent is to encourage the ones at home to continue there. I want to urge those who have an option to return home.

Anyone who doesn't want outside work, but is forced to it by financial circumstances or her husband's decision has a real challenge. A dear friend of years ago wanted very much to stay at home with her third child. She had a deeply rooted feeling of bitterness against her husband for making her work and justified flirtations with other men because of it. Eventually, she sacrificed the family to her bad attitude.

If you really want to stay at home but cannot, you must be careful to guard your heart and develop a good attitude. Remembering that He is in charge of your life, ask the Lord to make a way of escape. You should discuss the desire of your heart with your husband without reflecting negatively upon him as the provider. *Perhaps* he will consider the alternatives with you.

Studying your budget, careful planning and spending, getting out of debt, and home industry to supplement his income may enable the two of you to set new goals. Maybe one of them would be for you to leave your job.

Learn to live on his salary by displaying frugality while you are still working. It will help convince him that you could manage nicely if you stay at home. If he doesn't agree, you might remind him how hard it is to be super career woman—homemaker-mother-cook-laundress-maid. Discuss ways he could help you at home so both of you can function better.

Each husband and wife must decide what is best for their family and its particular situation. It takes careful management to maintain your role in the home. If you are in the marketplace now, I encourage you to begin looking for ways to make ends meet on your husband's salary so you can return home.

One very important but often overlooked aspect of a woman's being at home is what we pass on to following generations. All children need ideals and knowledge of God's structure of the home. Even those who have one parent or no parents need role models to guide them as a light set on a hill. I remember so well that when our children arrived home from school I was often downstairs ironing or otherwise occupied. "Mom?" they would yell. As soon as they heard my reply, all was well. They didn't have to see me; they only needed to know I was there.

TV cannot do it, nor will VCR's or making them lock the doors and stay inside. Having someone else there won't do it either. No one can take the place of a mom.

The same may be true for your husband; he might enjoy just knowing you're there. No matter where Wes traveled, when he called home he liked to hear my southern drawl answer the phone. He liked to know I was there polishing the anchor and holding it all together while he was away. That kind of security frees a man to attend to his duties with a quiet sense of peace.

If you **must** have a career, be sure you and your husband are in complete harmony about it. Having his support is critical to any project you might desire to do outside the home. It lets you know that you have the Lord's direction.

When our youngest child was in college, my responsibilities had narrowed considerably. The homefront was quiet. The governor's office called, asking me to consider an appointment to a position pertaining to children and education. I couldn't believe it. I can tell you I was terrified of the very thought.

The governor personally asked me to be on the Georgia Board of Education. I looked at him and said, "I'm not qualified."

"Oh, yes, you are. You're exactly what I want. You love children. I think you are a woman with strong convictions and will take a stand for what you believe," he said. Wes pointed his finger at me and said, "Bernie, it's perfect for you. You should do it."

There is nothing glamorous about a public service job. You think about the responsibilities much of the time. You read volumes of paperwork, some important and some empty. You are abused verbally, by letters, and by newspapers. Men take advantage of their size and vocal strength to put a woman in her place, especially when they disagree on an issue. It was new to me, all of it.

During seven years of service, I sometimes wept privately and often experienced rejection. Most of the time, I felt like a stump standing in the way of some wrong action. What I really wanted was to be as pervasive as kudzu, that fast-growing, never-to-be-stopped ground cover often seen in Georgia. I wanted to infect my new area of responsibility with sound thinking. It was tough!

One thing saw me through when I didn't think I would make it. Because my husband gave me the freedom to serve, I knew I was where the Lord wanted me even without achieving the results I desired.

He did not speak to me out of a cloud; He directed me through the word of my husband. When Wes was troubled by the amount of time I was involved in the job, he remembered his decision. If he gave the word, he knew I would resign just as quickly as I had followed his advice about accepting the position.

Here are two clues to help in talking to your husband and seeking an answer at decision-making time, ask him to think and pray about the situation and not answer immediately. Next, when you approach him, outline the *worst* case you can describe. When you forecast the worst and everything goes better, both of you are pleasantly surprised. Many wives make projects outside the home sound easy before accepting them. When the going gets rough, they don't understand their husbands' reactions. Don't be deceptive, even about seemingly insignificant issues. Men notice and suspect more serious deceptions.

At the center of God's will is the best place to be! It goes beyond reasonable, rational thinking. We must be in His presence and experience His peace to know we are there. Please seek His will about any activity you may be considering. Know in your heart that to perform it you won't have to leave your first love, the Lord, nor your second, your husband.

A capable, intelligent and virtuous woman, who is he who can find her? She is far more precious than jewels, and her value is far above rubies or pearls.

—Proverbs 31:10

14
Pitfalls to Progress

$\mathcal{I}$n my endeavor to cooperate with the Lord and become the wife He wants me to be, I have to guard against a number of pitfalls. Let's examine them together. Perhaps you will see one or two in your life you need to eliminate.

NAGGING

No one ever plans to nag, but it can become an unconscious habit that takes many forms. It's uncomfortable to realize that you are a nagger. It's unpleasant and something I'm sure you'd like to give up. "It is better to dwell in a corner of the housetop [on the flat oriental roof, exposed to all kinds of weather] than in a house shared with a nagging, quarrelsome *and* faultfinding woman" (Proverbs 21:9). That unattractive trait doesn't need a lot of practice to become a habit and is often disguised as friendly reminders or spiritual encouragements.

First of all, ask the Lord to reveal if you are a nagger and if so, **why** you are one. Are you one who simply cannot say it one time? Your husband feels he's always being nipped at. He gets that defensive expression on his face again.

"Honey, I'm going to say this for the last time," you say, but you both know it's not true. If the Lord shows you that this is a problem area, it can be quickly corrected. Men don't mind being swallowed by a whale, but they hate being nibbled to death by minnows!

Sit down and share with your husband: "The Lord has shown me that I am a nagger and I realize it's wrong. I want you to enjoy being with me. I ask your forgiveness and would like you to help me break the habit." I'm confident he will be delighted to offer a few suggestions.

When children are involved, you should ask their forgiveness as well. If you've been nagging their dad, I'm sure it has spread to other members of the family. What they say about it may be shocking, but once convinced you mean business, they can be quite keen on helping mom overcome. With a proper agreement the family can signal you in kindness when you drift into the old pattern of showing irritation, harping on a subject, or making a request harshly.

"He who guards his mouth and his tongue keeps himself from troubles" (Proverbs 21:23). Being aware of these annoying tendencies, you can make some resolutions to aid you in conquering them. One way of breaking an old habit is to replace it with a new one. Train yourself to make a comment one time and no more, especially with your husband. With children, according to their ages, repetition is often part of training. Your goal with them is to say it once and have them obey. Husbands and children don't always listen to repetitious comments. They think, Same old program—I'm changing stations. They may look right at you, but they don't hear you.

Express it and forget it; your responsibility is over. It is then your husband's responsibility to act or not to act upon your request. Choose a different approach, the habit of kindness. "She opens her mouth with skillful and godly Wisdom, and in her tongue is the law of kindness—giving counsel and instruction" (Proverbs 31:26). "A gentle tongue [with its healing power] is a tree of life, but willful contrariness in it breaks down the spirit" (Proverbs 15:4).

I'm not speaking about not being what you are. You may be like me, a verbally expressive person. According to articles I've read, women, by design, use more words than men. Make a concerted effort to be sure what you say is important enough to be said—that it has worth and is not unkind.

Is your objective to move your husband to action and have you mistakenly begun to believe your demands are what do it? When you probe with a sharp, nagging tongue, he will react according to his temperament. He may move but not very far, and he'll stay there until you make him uncomfortable again. Your husband's reason for acting might be to maintain peace and bring an end your constant reminders. If so, you'll have to go through the same routine the next time you think he should do something. It becomes a vicious cycle for both of you, and you are no nearer your goal of encouraging him to be a man of action.

Doesn't this sound like an unpleasant way of life? I'm sure you don't really believe your husband would never take out the garbage unless you nag him about it. I've drifted toward that kind of routine but recognized it and turned away when I did. The Lord can and will move your husband in the best direction for your good (Romans 8:28-29).

One lady asked me if "encouragement" involved mentioning what needed to be done or admonishing her husband when he doesn't do the things he should. Because there are so many combinations of temperament, gifts, and backgrounds, no formulas can guarantee a certain result in the husband-wife relationship. The only **set** formula that works for our good and God's glory is to read the Book and do it His way. Ask the Lord to reveal His wisdom about particular situations. He will *not* show you a way which *isn't* in accordance with His Word.

Encouraging and nagging are very different. Find out what appeals most to your man. Do quiet talks in the late evening work best? Is he an early bird who doesn't mind talking in the morning? Carefully choose those times to share what's on your mind. Always use kind wording and avoid accusation or absolute expressions such as never and always.

With some men, making an appointment to discuss problems works very well. If you have earned the reputation of **not** being a nagger, he'll be more approachable and more likely to listen. You can tackle any subject with an underlying sense of humor, and he will really appreciate it. If you desire to be one with him, growing together, he will know and you will benefit. Bathe everything in prayer before you begin, then you'll have quiet confidence in the

Lord's leadership and know the results will be His. Be prepared spiritually to accept the outcome whatever it may be.

The preventive measures are thought and planning. Plan to be an encourager and not a nagger. Be kind, thoughtful, creative, and make a commitment once and for all. You'll be tested and tempted to return to the old habits, but remember your commitment and choose correctly again.

IGNORING HIS ADVICE

If you have nagged your husband into doing or saying something, you can never feel sure his guidance is from the Lord. Whether your husband is a Christian or not, the Lord will guide you through him. Just don't try to manipulate him to say what you think you need.

For most of my life I've had a problem with aching feet. It started when I was very young, and it was difficult to find properly fitting shoes. My parents could not afford them, besides we lived in an area where good shoes were not readily available. Several doctors tried to help me by prescribing strange-looking shoes, which I disliked intensely.

I eventually consulted with an orthopedic surgeon in Atlanta. As I stood there looking at the x-rays, tears crept down my face. I saw why my feet hurt so much—my bones were crooked. It didn't take an expert to read the x-rays. In an effort to compensate, my toes had turned improperly, putting a lot of pressure on the joints. I knew what Dr. Willingham would recommend.

"How can I know this is what God wants me to do?" I asked.

119

"That's simple," he said, "we'll just ask Him right now." Standing in a circle with him, his nurse, and my daughter, Kandy, we prayed.

When Wes came in from work, I was excited to tell him about my appointment. I explained the proposed surgical procedure as best I could. He wasn't happy about it. Days went by, and he said nothing. One afternoon, I asked Kandy if she thought I should mention it again. I didn't want to nag him, yet I was anxious to have a *word from the Lord*. Kandy suggested I wait awhile longer.

"Guess who I sat by at Rotary Club today?" Wes asked that very night when he came home. It's a large club and he enjoys meeting new men every week. He had joined some men at a table and as usual introduced himself.

"Hi, I am Bob Willingham. I believe I am your wife's doctor," responded the man beside him. Sitting right there Dr. Bob drew a diagram of my feet on a napkin. He explained the operation and the reasons he thought surgery was necessary.

You may not agree with me, but I think the Lord is interested in every detail of our lives. He will honor the smallest commitment to obedience for His glory as He honored mine about not nagging. He again answered me through my husband, without my intervention or manipulation. The surgery was a painful experience, but the results were well worth the weeks of recovery. During the most trying times, I was comforted by knowing the Lord had given us guidance. Wes had not been in favor of the surgery, but the Lord changed his heart for my good.

PUSHING

To progress in your relationship with your husband, it's important to stimulate him with encouragement. Don't try pushing him into some job, place, or relationship beyond his capabilities or gifts. You'll only succeed in making him feel like a failure. Then, you can be sure he'll think and act like one. He will bring to fruition the feeling he has about himself.

Be careful of what you say. "Look, honey, at the bracelet Don gave Sally. He must really love her." Planting little seeds about possessions is unwise. You are pushing him to dissatisfaction, but not in the right way. There is a fine line between encouraging a man and pushing him too far or into being what he does not want to be. Setting up a goal he cannot achieve will make you unhappy because he will be unhappy.

Part of receiving your husband is to accept that he may not feel as driven as you do or as ambitious as you wish he would be. I don't know what type man you are living with, but you can't change him. If you want him to achieve his utmost, encourage, love, and stimulate him; work with him in every way possible, but beware of pushing too hard or too much. It can make him into a very miserable man, and you'll pay the price right along with him. You may get a glimpse of somewhere the Lord is taking the two of you. Pray about it, but don't jump ahead of His timing and mess it all up. Remember Sarah and Abraham—doing God's will *their* way.

Comparing

Comparing your husband to other men, fictional or real, is not creative encouragement. The results are usually defensive maneuvers and an emotional barrier emerging between you. Every time he looks at another woman, you may feel unfavorably compared. When he admires a dress, a hairdo, or a career of another woman, you may feel discouraged, rejected, inefficient, ineffective, inadequate, short-changed, or mistreated. It doesn't feel good, does it? Please don't use his behavior or comments as justification for your behavior. Instead, teach him to speak the language of love by demonstration. He is accountable for himself.

We live in a world of comparison. When you read and hear about the modern men who supposedly do 50 percent of the home work and child care, your focus might shift to all the things your husband doesn't do rather than what he does. You can only ruin your opportunity to be the wife God wants you to be if you compare your husband to such men privately or publicly.

"However, when they measure themselves with themselves and compare themselves with one another, they are without understanding *and* behave unwisely" (II Corinthians 10:12b). If you *feel* negative because of your husband's comparisons, don't blurt it out when you're angry. Discuss it with him at an appropriate time, saying how it makes you feel without accusing him. Are you careful to notice and comment about his thoughtful gestures that make you feel good about yourself and your relationship? If so, you are in a far better position to have his listening ear when you have an appeal.

My dad didn't know anything about feminists or the present-day movement for women's rights, but if mom was late getting home, he started dinner. He was no sissy; he saw a need and met it. He frequently got up earlier than Mom and brought her coffee in bed. I took it for granted until I didn't receive the same service after I was married. I didn't realize that ways of ministering vary with individuals. Perhaps your husband doesn't do the same kind of things another husband does. Don't compare, and you'll be happier. If something is bothering you, pray for him about it. Opportunities may arise to discuss the problem, but do it without expectation of change. If it happens, let it be a pleasant surprise and not simply a meeting of your expectation.

If your husband doesn't remember your birthday or fix the leaky faucet, telling him about your best friend's husband who is so thoughtful will not increase his sensitivity. You can help it to develop by sharing in a spirit of love about your feelings when he makes a thoughtful gesture.

The reason I use such illustrations is so that you might relate to them, not to compare. Comparison is one way women get into trouble. It drags down your spirit. We can always find someone who is worse off than we are, and there are always those who are better, prettier, or possess more. We choose our comparisons according to the day. If we're a little down, it's those whom we consider enviable. If we are feeling up, we compare ourselves with those to whom we feel superior. Comparison is unwise, except when we compare ourselves to God's standard—where does the Lord want me to be?

Your husband may struggle with his own thoughts about comparison—looks, abilities, and promotions or recognitions others receive. Don't make him more uncomfortable by having to deal with your subtle or obvious comparisons as well.

NEGATIVE PERSUASION

Saying to your husband he doesn't love you is a sure way to shoot yourself in the foot. When you are aggravated, do you ever say, "If you really loved me, you wouldn't do that."? Or "If you really loved me, you would . . . "? When such statements are made often enough, you may convince him that what you're saying is true. He may decide he doesn't love you or does not know how to love. I was guilty of sending that message in many ways—verbally and otherwise. I knew it wasn't accomplishing anything. I was frustrated with myself. A change needed to take place, but it took time for me to break a bad habit.

One night in a Chinese restaurant, Wes's fortune cookie said: "You have a great potential for loving." When he wasn't looking, I sneaked the little piece of paper into my purse. I wanted to project to Wes the truth of this message. I wanted to be the object of the love he could give. Its next appearance was on his mirror. He would look at it many mornings to follow. Perhaps I should have inserted the words "Wes has—" and placed it on my mirror.

Convince your husband of how great he is as a lover, as a husband, and then hang around to be the recipient—in case it is forthcoming. People tend to project back to you the characteristics you confirm in them. You cannot expect a positive response from your husband if you give him negative input. Many husbands, fathers, and men in general have come to believe they can't understand women, are unable to meet their needs, and are incapable of loving the women in their lives. It is our fault to some degree. There is nothing in the Scriptures that says a man can't understand his wife. We need to change this negative thinking.

A daddy whose daughter was going through an extended rebellious spell, asked me if I had felt secure and loved by my Dad.

"How did he do it?" he continued. It was a difficult question to answer. We went over the usual reasons—physical gestures of affection, thoughtful deeds, time spent together. He had made all those efforts, but his daughter still had a problem *feeling* he loved her. I'm incapable of loving was his conclusion

"Don't accept that idea," I was happy to tell him. He was capable of loving and did love. God is love, and Jesus, who is God, is living in the born-again. We most certainly have the capacity to love and do love. We may be missing the step of communicating it to the recipient, or the recipient may be failing to receive the love we offer.

Perhaps you should quit assuming your *feelings* are correct and look at the relationships in your home from God's point of view. Your children should be able to learn how to convey love by observing you. If they don't get the message from dad, by all means let it come from mom's behavior. Make sure those around you learn how to love by watching you, especially your husband.

EXPECTING

Expecting something is a sure way to be disappointed. It stymies growth in your relationship. "He who expects nothing is never disappointed," or so Wes says. If you load your husband or friends with expectations, you can fully expect to be disappointed. But if you lay them before the Lord, you can be confident they are in good hands. He knows you intimately and will fulfill those expectations which are for your good.

You have a legitimate need for intimacy in your life. Ideally, your husband should be your closest friend. If he isn't, don't look to another man to meet the need. Seek out and ask the Lord to help you find a special girlfriend with whom to have a close friendship. Take all your needs to the Lord.

Many women expect to be mothers, but the Lord doesn't allow some to experience motherhood. Maybe you are one of them. You have done everything you can, medically and otherwise and have sought help in every way possible. It seems an insurmountable problem because it's happening to you. The Lord is taking care of that expectation, saying, "Wait, it is not time," or "You, dear, are not going to bear children. You can be the mother of many spiritual children if you will be available for My will" (see Isaiah 54:1).

All of us have an intimate area in which we hurt sometimes. Maybe we are unable even to express it to anyone else. Remember, "for no temptation—no trial regarded as enticing to sin [no matter how it comes or where it leads] has overtaken you *and* laid hold on you that is not **common** to man" (I Corinthians 10:13a, emphasis added). To know others are suffering in the same way may not be a comfort, but the comfort is in knowing that He who loves you most will care for your expectations.

"He will [always] also provide the way out—the means of escape to a landing place—that you may be capable *and* strong *and* powerful patiently to bear up under it" (I Corinthians 10:13b). "My soul, wait only upon God *and* silently submit to Him; for my hope *and* expectation are from him" (Psalm 62:5). The Lord is the One to meet your needs. He may do it through others, but He is in control, and you cannot decide how He will do it.

How well I remember when I **truly** gave my expectations to the Lord. It was our anniversary. Wes said nothing that morning, but late in the afternoon a flower arrangement arrived with a simple note. My immediate thought was a familiar one. Sure, he forgot our anniversary until now. Quickly following came a reminder of my commitment about expectations. Turning from those negative thoughts, I chose gratitude for receiving such a nice remembrance.

Wes came in the door after work with a small, beautifully wrapped package in his hand. Since I no longer expected anything, the little girl in me came out, and I giggled and jumped up and down with excitement. Wes could readily see that something was different.

"You really didn't expect anything, did you?" he asked with surprise in his voice. I could honestly answer that I didn't.

Your husband may or may not enjoy giving you gifts and remembering you in special ways for special days. Your response when he does will in large measure determine whether he will continue. Your gratitude will mean a lot to him. If you constantly expect and he doesn't deliver, you are going to stay disappointed. It will show, and you'll be further from resolution than ever.

If your husband gives you a dress that is the wrong color or just not what you had in mind, wear it anyway. If it is the wrong size and you exchange it, he understands . . . probably . . . maybe. . . . You suppress his desire to give if you insist on taking gifts back or exchanging them without an obvious-to-him reason. If the flowers are pink and your room is peach, display them anyway. Show an attitude of gratefulness for whatever your husband gives you.

I have heard many wives discussing their husbands' lack of thoughtfulness. Asking about their past was revealing. Several had hurt their husbands early in marriage by returning gifts; others had exchanged them unnecessarily or had shown a critical spirit. If you have ever done any of that, beseech the Lord to show you your responsibility, and then go to your husband and ask forgiveness.

I don't say your husband isn't thoughtful because you behaved that way. Maybe he has never given you a gift. Some men are not thoughtful, and your behavior has nothing to do with it, but there is a good possibility you knew about it before you married him. Generally speaking, he didn't change when he walked down the aisle and back again.

You are the one who changed; you accepted his thoughtlessness before marriage. I have heard there are some men who change as soon as they say "I do," but it isn't a common occurrence. Usually the wife believes she can get him to change.

Expectations may be in other areas. Maybe he doesn't speak up on issues when you wish he would. He's too quiet; when the children are misbehaving he doesn't correct them at all or at least not the way you wish he would; he doesn't actively try to get a better job or better pay. Thinking about the times you're disappointed and feel you haven't gotten what you deserve will reveal whether you are placing expectations on your husband.

When you recognize your inappropriate attitudes, think of the burden you put on him that he shouldn't have to bear. He should be looking unto the Lord to please Him. You may be distracting him with your demands. He has felt their weight all along but may not even realize it or know how to express his distress. Enter into his burden when you ask his forgiveness and he will feel your remorse.

ALWAYS HAVING YOUR SAY

Butting in is resented by anyone, especially husbands. If yours is talking and you see the opportunity to make a joke, commenting at his expense isn't welcome. It may be funny to others and temporarily amusing to you, but to him, it is hurtful. Usually such jokes are demeaning and publicly expose a trait best discussed privately, if at all.

I heard someone speak on the subject of a man loving his wife as he loves his own body. If a man had an ugly scar on his chest, he wouldn't open up his shirt to show it off but would conceal it as much as possible. That should be our attitude toward our husbands' weaknesses. Should you expose your husband's scars even in private much less in public? He may use that technique on you to make others laugh, but don't retaliate. Don't use public display or sarcasm to send a message to your mate.

A high level executive told me he preferred his wife to converse socially without discussing the business. He didn't say his wife was not intelligent, knowledgeable, or a good conversationalist. He wanted others to know his wife thinks he is capable and smart in his area of expertise. He never wanted to feel intimidated by her.

I have been in groups where a wife talked about business. Her comments often seem to imply that she doesn't think her husband is doing the right thing and that she could do it better —or he could if he would only listen to her. Butting in on business matters and conversations communicates an improper attitude. No man likes that.

JEALOUS DEMONSTRATIONS

The best defense you have against other women is a good offense. For a blood-washed, born-again wife that means becoming all God wants you to be and all that He says you are. Retaliation, comparing, nagging, and catty remarks won't correct your husband's behavior. He will only sulk or perhaps blast you verbally. He may stay away from home. Acting jealous makes an undesirable situation worse and is always unprofitable. Instead, choose a proper time to talk over your feelings in a **non-accusing** manner.

Jealousy of time your husband spends with other men is equally unprofitable. It may be important to him, so encourage him to participate in the right kind of men's activities, such as Bible classes and prayer groups. He should be free to develop relationships of fun, fellowship, and friendship with men of character.

There is no place males can go today that women cannot enter. Their clubs, the marketplace, the sports arena—all have been invaded by females. Yet we women have our own special endeavors that exclude men. They can't have babies, breast feed, and *feel* like women. They need to *feel* like men and be in situations where they are sensitive to the differences between the sexes.

Some men are trying to become women. They can be changed surgically and hormonally or wear women's apparel, but none of that can alter what the hand of God has designed. What awful bondage, in not wanting to be what and who God created them to be. Allow your husband to enjoy his masculinity just as you should enjoy being feminine.

He may also need time to be alone to read and think or be involved in a hobby. He has to have special times with his sons and grandsons. Guard his schedule so he is free to enjoy those times. Make it easy for him to participate in man talk and sports or hobbies. Your supportive attitude will be a great help.

No matter how carefully disguised, jealousy is ugly. It always comes out as a nasty attitude. Make the decision not to be jealous!

FEAR

Fear of taking a risk is certain to keep a man from getting ahead. Is your husband a hostage to your fear of any kind of change? It is a subtle form of manipulation.

The hardy spirit of a pioneer woman would be handy for us modern women in taking risks and facing possible failure. You must allow your husband to work at what he loves, even if it involves risks. If he never changes jobs and your family never moves, you may attain security, but he could lose initiative and enterprise. Deterring him from vocational choices by limiting his options may also gain you security, but you'll have a very unhappy man at your house. The Scriptures speak of having a gentle and quiet spirit. We are not to be anxious about anything—not to get hysterical about life's circumstances. But what about getting excited over a new adventure?

Are you embarrassed about your husband's vocation or proud of him regardless of what he does? A young man we know well is a mechanic. He's a good one and prides himself on his work. He is always looking for ways to improve it. But no matter how hard he scrubs, his hands keep a residue of grease. Nevertheless, his wife is loyal and proud of him. They have a close relationship. Would you judge him to be a success? I surely do, and I am confident his wife and children do, too.

I particularly remember a nice, ambitious young man from another part of the country. He was transferred to Atlanta for an impressive promotion. His family moved into a lovely house. All seemed well until I was told that they were returning to their former home. I couldn't understand, but Wes explained. The wife had been unable to adjust. She wanted to be back home with her folks where she'd lived all of her life. Her wishes came before her husband's career, so he chose to take a demotion and keep his marriage intact. I admire him for that choice, but it made me wonder how many wives are holding their husbands captive to their personal desires. Years later, I learned that the couple divorced. "I was miserable!" he said.

Surely a wife lacks love and respect for her husband if she hinders his progress. That same wife may be impatient with her husband's lack of ambition and entirely blind to the fact she is the source of the problem. She'll also miss the money he could have made in a more advanced position.

Are you encouraging your husband to do the work he does best and excel at it? If you're causing him to stand still because you enjoy the security of sameness, you can set aside all your fears. The Lord has equipped you to meet any new challenge. "For God did not give us a spirit of timidity—of cowardice, of craven and cringing and fawning fear—but [He has given us a spirit] of power and love and of calm *and* well-balanced mind *and* discipline *and* self-control"(II

Timothy 1:7). "Do not fret *or* have any anxiety about anything, but in every circumstance *and* in everything by prayer and petition [definite requests] with thanksgiving continue to make your wants known to God" (Philippians 4:6).

Confess your fears and anxieties to the Lord, and then let your husband know you're laying them aside. Ask his forgiveness, and commit yourself to supporting him in all ways.

UNFORGIVING SPIRIT

Unforgiveness is something people rarely admit they are troubled by, yet I have met some who carry it about like a trophy. Until that attitude is transformed, healing won't come.

"I can forgive, but I will never forget" is something I often hear. Anyone who makes that statement will not forget. Most of the time, forgiveness won't take place either. An unforgiving spirit brings hurt, suffering, bitterness, and contagion that spreads to all with whom it comes in contact. It can be a root cause for the habit of nagging.

Learning to forgive was a difficult struggle for me and seemed beyond my power until I grasped the truth: forgiveness is impossible until you are born again. Then all things are possible because "I am a new creation, old things are passed away." The Christ Who lives in me can forgive through me. That is exciting news!

I made a commitment to God. "Lord, I cannot forgive him. I do not really believe he deserves my forgiveness," I prayed. "But I know you love and forgive him and You live in me. Today I choose to be willing for You to forgive him through me." Then I rested in Jesus to do the good work which He had begun. I didn't mention to Wes or anyone else what I was doing, but every time I felt offended or hurt, I breathed that prayer.

I was seated in my dressing room with the door closed when one of our daughters came into our bedroom.

"You sure look pretty," her dad impulsively remarked. I could almost hear his brain working as he realized he was complimenting her on a quality the Lord had made. "But if I could wish one thing for you, it would be that you have a forgiving spirit like your mother's," he added.

Wow, was I happy to hear that comment! I needed to overhear that conversation. I had felt the Lord was making forgiveness a reality in me, but the exciting part was being allowed to see it becoming real to those around me.

I was home alone when the Lord brought to my remembrance a time when I had severely disciplined Jamey, our oldest daughter. Her misbehavior had been more childish misjudgment than willful disobedience. My problem was anger, and I reacted according to my inconvenience. I could hardly wait for her to arrive home from school so I could ask her to sit down with me. Without details, I asked her forgiveness for a time I had over disciplined her in anger.

"I don't remember your ever doing that, but yes, I forgive you," she said. And off she went.

"Mom, the other day I remembered a time you were really mad at me and disciplined me," Jamey told me several years later. "I began to feel angry and hurt as I thought about the incident. Then I remembered, Oh, yes, Mom asked me to forgive her and I did! I want you to know how much it meant to me."

Recently when Wes and I were teaching about forgiveness, I recalled that conversation, and a deeper truth came through. Jamey didn't feel better because I asked her forgiveness. She felt relief from her own unforgiveness because she had chosen to forgive! That is true freedom, available to you and me every day if we choose to forgive. We do not have to wait on others to ask our forgiveness; we can be free from unforgiveness right now. If you're caught in the aftermath of old hurts, choose forgiveness.

WHAT PITFALLS ARE IN YOUR WAY?

As we have walked through this list, perhaps you have identified one or more problems in your relationship. To continue developing as the wife of a successful husband, you must eliminate the pitfalls to progress.

For I have learned how to be content (satisfied to the point where I am not disturbed or disquieted) in whatever state I am. I know how to be abased and live humbly in straitened circumstances, and I know also how to enjoy plenty and live in abundance.

—Philippians 4:11b,12a

15
On the Road Again

$\mathcal{J}$f something isn't a little difficult, there is no need to be adaptable. But what if your husband came in one day and said the family must move? "On the road again" is the theme of many families today. It can result in insecure feelings. Prepare yourself and don't allow them. Your attitude and reaction set the direction for everyone in your house.

We were living in an attractive, comfortable home in Baton Rouge, although we had discussed a larger home for our growing family. Wes returned from a trip to Atlanta to see the top level people. We always enjoyed a happy time when he came home from a trip. After everyone had hugged his legs, his arms, his knees, and had given the embraces children do, we had a little quiet time. "Bernie," Wes said, "you know the big house you want? Well, I'm going to buy it for you."

"Really? Wow!"

"There's only one little catch; it will be in Atlanta."

It wasn't an unusual situation for us. We had moved several times during our nine years of marriage. If we stayed somewhere over two years, I began to get restless. Moving is a great way to have clean closets.

In hindsight, we were blessed because of our moves far beyond the obvious boost to my husband's career. When the company transferred him from Augusta to Baton Rouge, we moved to within an hour's drive of my parents' home. Nine months later my dad died at the young age of fifty. That move was a bonus because it allowed me to be near him before his death. Those months were important in building memories and increasing the good times my dad had with the young grandchildren he adored.

With the promotion to Atlanta three years later, we were within an hour's drive of Wes's parents. Five years after that his father died. I was able to help his mom by driving them to the doctor and to visit the hospital. The children enjoyed knowing Papa and playing in his vineyard. Wes was glad to have these years close to his dad and to be near when he was needed.

When a wife has a proper attitude, her husband is relieved and confident. Children seem to respond in accordance with their mom's response. She sets the tone for the entire family. To say moves are not difficult would be ridiculous, but that there are hidden benefits you cannot see at the moment is true. The Father's hand is in control, and He sees it all; He knows the end from the beginning. Looking at everything as coming from your Father's hand and knowing no other one cares as He does helps to keep joy intact in spite of your emotions.

If your family does move, be prepared to face all the necessary adjustments. Perhaps what you and your husband had expected at the new location is simply not coming to fruition. Your attitude as you face each issue will help or hinder him. Moves are expensive and ironically, promotions don't always mean a raise in pay, at least not immediately. Settling into a new neighborhood, a new house needing new draperies, different weather requiring different clothes; on and on the expenses grow.

Moving to Atlanta was difficult for us. We bought a house in Sandy Springs, but the owners couldn't move out for several weeks. Meanwhile, we stayed in a motel apartment. We had one week's supply of clothes each. Our furniture and other possessions were packed away in Louisiana. We had to register the children in a school that was on split sessions. We'd sold one of our cars, so I was a full-time chauffeur, driving Wes and the children somewhere all day it seemed.

Fall came, and our clothes weren't warm enough. The children had no place to play except a little playground that was nothing more than a plot of Georgia red clay. In between car trips, I could usually be found at the Laundromat. Diapers and a little boy's pants loved that red clay. My sister-in-law lent me an iron so I could occupy my extra time with the challenge of ironing on an upholstered chair seat.

With minimum utensils supplied by the apartment, my cooking took on a new shade of interest. Six weeks dragged by. If I was ever going to have a nervous breakdown, that would have been the time. A routine day might start with arising at four-thirty, waking the children, driving Wes to the airport, returning to get the children dressed for school, driving to Sandy Springs, and dropping the children at school.

I didn't like Atlanta very much, but I'm sure the difficult circumstances had a lot to do with it. My unpleasant feeling about the city lingered even after we were settled into our nice new home and the children were established in school. One day my cousin flew in for a visit. Shera looked toward the city as we drove in from the airport. The tallest building then was the Hyatt Regency, but coming from the flatlands of Louisiana, her reaction was, "Wow! what a skyline!" I looked at it and said, "Wow, what a skyline!" I had been blinded to the view because my vision was clouded by my circumstances. I love Atlanta now. I simply had to make a choice about my attitude. How much better for me and the family if it hadn't taken so long.

When you're in similar circumstances, you'll have to make the right choices, too, so be prepared to make those adjustments. You may return to an area, as I did when we went back to Baton Rouge the second time. Old friendships are not the same. You will probably make new friends, find a new church, and live in a different neighborhood. Don't expect sameness. You are growing and expanding. All kinds of new opportunities await you.

When we had been in our present home about a year, a head hunter began to talk with Wes about another job. I encouraged him to go for it.

"I can't believe you," said Kristi, our adopted college girl. "You have settled into this new home, your children are happy in school and you're saying it's okay to move?"

"Sure," I said, "there's a new adventure out there somewhere! I don't want to miss it if that's where the Lord wants us to be." I know Wes and the family liked this attitude much better, and he was free to make the best decision.

Look at change as a positive and seize each one as an opportunity to enrich your life. A smaller house can be an adventure and challenge to your creativity. Children are adaptable and will quickly reflect your responses to less money, fewer activities, and less time with Dad.

Your husband's new position may not be as prestigious as his former one. You are his most important support person as he adjusts to it. Assurance that you still hold him in high esteem is critical to his morale.

Your first priority is to find a new church. People there will help you and your children will make new friends. You'll find areas of ministry in which the Lord will enable you to participate. Families generally delay doing this, but it's key to an easier adjustment. As soon as you can, make your new home comfortable and attractive.

Make the right choice, and all of life can be fun. I've hated to leave each place we have lived. I missed my friends, and yet I always anticipated something new and exciting wherever we were going. I am an only child, grew up in a rural area of Louisiana, never traveled far away from my parents, but I've enjoyed moving around the southeast. I don't believe I'm so different from most women. We can always choose to have the correct attitude and gain much by making that choice. Look for the adventure in every move. Find the challenge in having to do something you don't want to do.

Only [do not let your] freedom be an incentive to your flesh and an opportunity or excuse [for selfishness], but through love you should serve one another.

—Galatians 5:13b

16
Profit From Loneliness

$\mathcal{H}$ow does a man feel when he returns from the battlefield of work at the end of the day to find his wife depressed and suffering from loneliness? I wouldn't enjoy the prospect, yet this is the greeting many husbands receive daily.

Everywhere I turn I bump into this enemy, loneliness. Many of my young college friends who are away from home are lonely. Many of my young married friends who are still in the baby business are lonely. Those of my own age who have grown children are lonely as are older women who are widows. Loneliness seems to be an acquaintance of us all at some time in our lives.

We describe it in many different ways, although we speak of the same feeling. You remember the strange gnawing sensations in the pit of your stomach when you entered a new place for lunch or a meeting. You didn't know where to sit and were unsure of your welcome. Even those of us who have bluffed through it know what that's like.

Some may call it depression, others emptiness. Whatever the description, the cause is generally the same—I *feel* sorry for myself. We girls are specialists in pity parties. It's a comfortable place to be; after all, we've been there often enough to feel at home.

Loneliness affects all of our society today. You can be in a sea of people, busy with much activity, and still feel lonely. Young people are committing suicide because of it. They see themselves as insignificant in their families and in their world. They deeply desire to be valued by at least one person, just as each of us does. Perhaps they do not know Jesus, or if they do, they don't realize who they are in Him. They haven't the security of the high esteem He places on them as individuals.

As a born-again you must strive to have an accurate picture of who you are in Christ. It's the only basis on which to combat loneliness. We humans have a legitimate need for intimate fellowship. When it's not met, we can be burdened with a sense of isolation. I believe that Jesus in His humanity expressed it when He asked the three disciples to remain wakeful and pray with Him in the Garden of Gethsemane. The Lord must have designed us to need one another. Why else would we be compared to a body whose different parts all rely on each other? When one part aches, all the rest of the body suffers. Why else would we be told to "bear (endure, carry) one another's burdens" (Galatians 6:2a)? Satan can use this very legitimate need to throw you into a pit of uncomfortable feelings when it's not met.

As Christians we should be in the ministry of bear hugging. Many in the body of Christ never get a hug. I hope you have friends and acquaintances who are helping to meet your need as you do theirs. Do you hug generously? You'll seldom give a hug without receiving one in return.

Identify the problem accurately when you're feeling blue—a need not being met, your monthly cycle, allowing the comments of others to put you in the depths of loneliness. "You poor thing, your husband always works. You are so tied down with the children. Don't you ever have any time for yourself? You look tired."

Is the Lord giving you times alone for constructive thinking about your goals, home, husband, and Him? It's important to your spiritual and emotional well-being. This could be your golden opportunity to spend more time with the Lord. Maybe your Bible has been gathering dust. What about the new book you bought months ago and in which you will find a wealth of encouragement.

I think my mom found the cure for loneliness years ago. She sets a great example of practicing the cure. Mom lives alone in a rural area of Louisiana but seldom is lonely. She sews, cooks, freezes vegetables, and does handcraft projects, but that's only her busy work. Her cure is that she focuses not on herself but on others. I hardly ever see my mom that she isn't involved in giving of herself. The thrust of most of her projects is outreach. Most of her sewing is for someone else. The canning is for gifts to me and her grandchildren. She often cooks dishes for the church or for a bereaved family. I know she has washed down the outside of the church, worked in the cemetery, upholstered church bus seats, helped someone paint, garden, can, or quilt. She ministers to many of the practical needs in the community. She makes friends with all ages and is interested in them as individuals. Her greatest gift to all she meets is herself. Do people like her? You better believe it.

"Give, and [gifts] will be given you, good measure, pressed down, shaken together and running over will they pour into [the pouch formed by] the bosom [of your robe and used as a bag]. For with the measure you deal out—that is, with the measure you use when you confer benefits on others—it will be measured back to you" (Luke 6:38). The lack you sense in your own life probably is the area where you need to give something away. This principle works in the manner of a conveyor belt. What you give away returns to you so you can give again. Be careful not to expect reciprocation from the one you give to. The Lord will see to your reimbursement in His way, from His resources, and in His time. He gives that we may give, not for us to keep. Our motive is important; we are not to give to get. If you lack love in your life—or fellowship or bear hugs—maybe you aren't giving enough to others.

The Lord wants to take your loneliness and turn it into victory. He wants to use your suffering to benefit others. "Blessed [be] the God and Father of our Lord Jesus Christ, the Father of sympathy (pity and mercies) and the God [Who is the Source] of every consolation *and* comfort *and* encouragement; Who consoles *and* comforts *and* encourages us in every trouble (calamity and affliction) so that we may also be able to console (comfort and encourage) those who are in any kind of trouble or distress, with the consolation (comfort and encouragement) with which we ourselves are consoled *and* comforted *and* encouraged by God" (II Corinthians 1:3,4).

The Lord never wastes our personal experiences. He wants to console and comfort us so we might do likewise. He has someone ready to receive from us what He gives to us in our times of need. After a spiritual bout, look around. Someone is waiting to receive your gift of service, your love, your bear hug, or your encouraging words. He always has a source ready before a need is known. You are His channel for meeting someone else's need.

In a Bible class I attended, the teacher spoke about suffering. On the way home my girlfriend and I made light of the idea of present-day Christians suffering because we felt they were not acquainted with real suffering. You know what happened—the Lord made sure both of us became acquainted with it in the months ahead.

I had little sympathy for women who experienced depression or indulged in pity parties. After all, I thought, they could easily choose not to be in such an emotional state. I wasn't prepared for the blue funk of awakening one day with a big dark cloud over me. Everything seemed gray and colorless. I felt as though I would cry if anyone said a word to me.

I began to scrutinize my life to see if an unconfessed sin was lurking in my heart and causing this problem. What had I done? What was wrong with me? I was terribly distressed. A friend of ours came by several days later, and I told him about my terrible feelings, expressing my concern that I didn't understand.

"Trust in the Lord with all thine heart and lean not unto thine own *understanding*," he said with a smile. He advised me not to worry about what I didn't understand but to relax and see what there was to learn from it.

With this in mind, I chose to focus on the Lord. I memorized the twenty-third Psalm and for the next few days concentrated on all the different aspects of that passage of Scripture. I quoted it to the Lord with every inflection and deeper meaning I could find. I have to tell you the blue feelings didn't go away immediately, but they eventually did, and strangely, I almost missed the gray clouds. Something special happened between me and the Lord during my lonely time. Instead of running to your best friend for comfort, turn to the Lord and inquire as to His purpose. You've probably already guessed what happened next. The Lord brought several women into my life who were going through a similar experience. For the first time I felt I had something of value to share with them.

Loneliness and depression *can be* rooted in self-centeredness, being alone too often, or the Lord wanting our undivided attention. If it is caused by a physical problem, He will lead you to a doctor. Persistent or frequent negative moods should be dealt with promptly.

Having a servant's heart is the cure. Giving yourself to others not only melts away loneliness but may bring healing into the lives of those whom you serve. Scripture counsels about esteeming others as better than ourselves, loving your neighbor as you love yourself, turning the other cheek, and forgiving without limit. It sounds as though the Christian life is one of giving 150 percent to 200 percent, doesn't it? How much more then is this true for husbands and wives? There are so many verses having to do with this special relationship, which should be a primary example of giving oneself for another.

Whatever state you are in, the Lord is teaching you to be a servant. Training camps always mean hard times. We learn most in the boot camps of life, at least in the ones where we are truly trained.

"For the time being no discipline brings joy but seems grievous *and* painful, but afterwards it yields peaceable fruit of righteousness to those who have been trained by it—a harvest of fruit which consists in righteousness, [that is, in conformity to God's will in purpose, thought and action, resulting in right living and right standing with God]" (Hebrews 12:11).

God has a plan for you and for me. He won't neglect you no matter how small you feel. Don't waste your life fretting about where you are and pining for the future, the past, or easier times.

Choose to get up each day with an attitude of "Father, I am reporting for duty. I may not be on call for anything but scrubbing commodes, changing diapers, running car pools, or doing errands for my husband, but allow me to see Your flowers which say You love me this day. Remind me to share them with others, and show me every opportunity to give myself to someone else. Use me in the lives of others."

What husband wouldn't joyfully look forward to coming home to a woman like that? What lessons he may learn from her example!

She makes for herself coverlets, cushions and rugs of tapestry. Her clothing is of linen, pure white and fine, and of purple [such as that of which the clothing of the priests and the hallowed cloths of the temple are made].

—Proverbs 31:22

17
Man Looks on the Outward

*D*id you know you make your strongest impression on someone in the first twenty-nine seconds he looks at you? Whatever study produced that statistic, there is more to a woman than meets the eye. It's a fact of life, however, that man looks on the outward. "For the Lord sees not as man sees; for man looks on the outward appearance, but the Lord looks on the heart." (I Samuel 16:7b). Men and women, boys and girls judge from what they see.

I had a continuous struggle with what Wes wanted of me. I thought I knew what he expected, yet I was often mistaken. He wouldn't verbalize his desires directly, so I had to second guess him. To get rid of misunderstandings, I wanted him to sit down with me and communicate exactly what he was thinking. I hated the feeling that I was disappointing him, even though he never actually said so.

He sometimes indicated he would have liked me to be different, never directly, but with a look, an expression, or an indirect comment.

Once or twice I encouraged him to give our relationship careful consideration while he was out of town. I suggested he write down some of his thoughts while he was away from me and could be more objective. He never responded to my request. I could say he forgot, or I could make excuses about his lack of time, but he probably just didn't want to do it. It wasn't in his heart, or it would have been in his schedule. He may have had reservations about my response or feared my reaction.

When we were on a company trip together, I picked up some of the hotel stationary and wrote topics across the tops of the sheets: Expectations, Image projection as Wes's wife, Irritating habits, Character Development, Projects, Time for Outside Interests, Outside Interests Direction or Limits, Goals, or Pet Peeves. As I handed them to Wes, I asked him once again, "Some time this week would you try to write down your thoughts on these subjects?" The week passed, and Wes acted as though he didn't notice the stack of papers. I was very disappointed but determined not to repeat the request.

We were on the flight home when he suddenly opened his briefcase and removed the papers I had given him. He didn't say a word but began to write. Of course, I was dying of curiosity. I still have the papers. They are a little worn after all these years, but occasionally I take them out to review the precise words he wrote for me. I will share with you the page entitled Image.

Good conservative clothes - hi quality classics
Good jewelry - lots of it (That was good news!)
Warm - Friendly - OPEN - Confident
A president's wife who knows who she is - but
  also, remembers where she came from.
Stays slender and fit
Good stylish hairstyle
Good manicure
Looks - WELL CARED FOR! because she is
  cared for.

Your husband, like my Wes, may be slow to respond and he may even resent when you probe his inner thoughts. You want to ask him, and yet you don't want to be vulnerable because you fear what he may say. But shouldn't you let yourself be open to this man you chose to spend your life with? The flip side is that he may be delighted that after so much time you still want to know what he is thinking. He may like knowing you are concerned about his desires for your life together.

Men in general like to see a woman project energy. They seem to have trouble dealing with a wife being sick. If you have a headache, what does your husband say? "Go take an aspirin." If you have a lingering headache, he may say, "Go to the doctor." He wants you well, doesn't he? You can feel taken for granted when this happens, thinking that he knows you cannot do all your work, take care of his needs and the children's, and have an up-beat attitude with a constant headache. Maybe he is being protective. Don't forget, every individual expresses love and concern differently, especially men.

We should care for our "temple" not only to please our husbands, to feel and look better, but also to please the Lord. Discipline in the care of our bodies is a witness to those who see us. Let's consider two important points.

First, we must examine old patterns of behavior. Satan knows our ways well and will use them to trip up our plans for change. Second, we must acknowledge that we cannot make consistent, lasting changes in our own strength. Only the Lord can do that. So confess the old habits, acknowledge the strongholds, and ask the Lord to reclaim those areas in the power of His Name. Each day acknowledge to Him your utter dependence upon Him for victory.

WEIGHT, EATING HABITS, EXERCISE

Ask me my age anytime, but leave my weight alone. Most people would say I have no weight problem—only my scales and I know for sure. Each of us has trials. Two of mine are physical. Walking is the best form of exercise for me, but I find every legitimate and illegitimate reason I can to keep from doing it. I have no excuse; I must make the choice.

My other weakness is ice cream. Well, the real problem is self-discipline in my eating habits. I read a great deal about dieting and exercise, and we have gradually made changes in the way we prepare food at home. Dining out is another story, but we're learning to be selective and careful. By educating yourself about food preparation and the more harmful items, you can change how you eat. Knowing the truth aids in making wise choices.

If your closet is overcrowded with several sizes of clothes, do something about it. You can stew over it, you can discuss it with friends, but until you take control, the closet will stay just as it is. You need to determine the size you should be to be healthy, then take steps to achieve your goal and give those oversize clothes away.

Select an understanding friend and ask her to share your burden. Tell her the commitment you are making about your diet and exercise. Maybe she (or your husband if it would be an encouragement to him) will enter a program with you to attack a correctable problem. Fluctuating weight contributes to poor health.

YOUR WARDROBE

A good wardrobe suitable for one's lifestyle can be achieved by everyone. Wes used to tell me that it's easy to look like a million if you have a million, but it takes talent to look like a million without it. It's not an easy job, especially with limited funds, but it certainly can be done.

Be creative and get busy; be open to ideas. If you don't sew, perhaps you should learn how or barter talents with some friends. However, even sewing can be expensive. You must be a wise planner and shopper.

Always know where you stand with the budget before going shopping. You may need to talk to your husband, and be sure to have your limits in mind. Shopping can be the devil's workshop. If you make a commitment to not overspend, not to charge what you can't pay for at billing time, and not to spend more than your husband would approve of, you are in for fun and a guiltless time of good investment.

Consult the Lord. When I go shopping now, I often am not really shopping but buying. I usually get right to the need and consult the Lord. I pray something like this: "Father, we have an hour. You know what I need, and if You want me to have it, it will be there. The price will be right, the fit great, and the color becoming. If You don't want me to have anything new, there is something in my closet that would do just as well."

Adopt the "love it or leave it" rule. It will help your closet space considerably. You won't have it crowded with items you bought but don't feel good about. It will also help your budget because you won't buy as much.

A good friend of mine teaches a course on how to dress on a shoestring, and there are many other such seminars available across the country. There are good books with practical advice on wardrobe and the wise investment of your money. Read them and glean pertinent suggestions for the whole family. Christians often neglect to be good stewards with their money when it comes to buying clothes. Don't let it be true of you.

Years ago Wes and I had a wonderful trip in store for us—a cruise with a large group of business associates. The ship had formal evening meals, and when information about the trip arrived, I was excited but concerned about my clothes. I knew the lack of cash at our house would allow very few purchases.

One of the family magazines displayed in the grocery store had a caption that caught my attention. "How to Dress Like Jackie for

Pennies," it read. I quickly purchased the magazine and was pleasantly surprised to learn that the secret was shopping at thrift stores.

I knew of none in Atlanta at that time. They were not all around as they are today. I looked through the telephone directories and found only one located in a most undesirable area of the city. My heart sank. I kept thinking about my need and about the magazine being in the right place at the right time to help. A close friend said she would be glad to go with me, and off we went.

I was not prepared for what we saw when we walked into the store. There were piles of clothes everywhere. As I cautiously began to search through them, a clerk approached. She looked me over and asked my size.

"It happens that we just received a donation from a lady, and I think they are all your size," she said.

Needless to say, I left the store well loaded. I was delighted there was someone my size somewhere in Atlanta who needed a tax write-off or got bored with her clothes. I stayed busy all afternoon. I could hardly wait to show Wes my treasures. When he got home, I held up a new ensemble, an attractive, modest swimsuit with matching cover-up. Not only was it a great looking outfit, it fit well and was Wes's favorite color. The cover-up was an attractive casual dress by itself.

"How do you like it?" I asked.

"I thought you recently bought a swimsuit," he replied with a dismayed expression on his face.

"I did, honey, but I just couldn't pass this up for $1.25," I replied. What a look of relief he gave me.

The other outfits were wonderful, too. After the cleaners finished they looked brand new. They fit beautifully, and I did feel dressed like Jackie. I had another reason to be smug as I received compliments on my clothes during the cruise. Once again I had felt God's providential care. He does care about our raiment and about how we look. He does care. I'm sure the Lord placed those clothes at the thrift store at precisely the right time for me. He had the magazine in the right place, too.

Expose yourself to good taste by reading and studying appropriate pictures. There is no excuse for anyone not to look the best she can. There is so much information and creative ideas available to aid you.

Choose classy ladies to observe. Watch carefully how they walk, talk, and their selection of clothes and hairstyles. Decide what it is about their looks and manners you find attractive. Learn to see beyond the obvious by looking for the subtle differences in the appearance of women who catch your attention. Are there qualities you can emulate or gestures you might adopt? Would it help to project more of who you are on the inside?

Confide in friends and ask questions of them. Do I look like me, or do I look like I'm pretending to be someone I am not? Having wise godly counsel and depending on the peace that passes all understanding in your heart, you'll be a wise shopper, a sharp dresser, and more accurately portray your inner self.

Even when your clothing budget increases, use wisdom, good counsel, and a lot of common sense when purchasing clothes. Many women become careless as the Lord blesses them with more income, but our responsibility and accountability increase as our resources do.

HAIRSTYLE

Men don't seem as intense about long hair as they used to, but some still love it. Fortunately for me, Wes is more interested in my hair looking clean, shiny, and youthful. Your husband may be like him, or he may be a man who equates spirituality with the length of your hair, or simply prefers it on you. Show deference to his taste. Of all the people in the world you want to please, it should be your husband. That alone may bring a desired compromise, but if he can't settle for anything less than long hair, go for it and do the best you can. It may call for ingenuity you were not aware you possessed.

Your objective is to sell your husband on how you can look your very best. After all, you are the "expression of his glory." Give him every opportunity to see you at your best. Ask the Lord to guide his heart toward the right result. Seek advice from available experts. Consider the shape of your face, your build, and the condition of your hair. You may be surprised to learn that the way he likes your hair is the best style for you.

Above all, keep your hair looking healthy, shiny, clean, and well-groomed. Experiment with styles, and always make sure your husband knows you are most interested in his response. You do recall how you tried so hard to please him during your courtship days, don't you?

Your choice is simple. Even if you fail to sell him on what is actually the best for you according to yourself and others, *choose* to please him! Receive his choice and do the very best you can. Think through your priorities and keep them in order.

HANDS

We can't do much to change our hands. Many of us would like to hide them. I'm familiar with that feeling. Well, you may be unable to change their shape, size, or texture but you can certainly make them look their best.

My nails are not as strong and healthy as I'd like, yet I frequently speak before groups and can't avoid displaying my hands. There are wonderful new products on the market, so with diligent care and dedication to the cause we all can have lovely nails. My advice is to learn to do your own nails no matter how much effort it takes. A beauty salon can be costly, and besides you should know how to make repairs quickly and easily and have the necessary supplies.

Use rubber gloves every time you put your hands in water and wear garden gloves if you work in the yard. Be lavish with hand lotion, and don't forget the old home remedy for rough hands. Rub them generously with petroleum jelly and slip socks over them at night (great for softer feet, too). Even though I don't protect my hands and nails consistently, I know it's important.

I take care of my hair and nails much of the time, but that doesn't mean all women should. Many simply are not inclined that way. Learning to do a minimal amount of skillful care will make you more independent of outside help. It will also help in times when a salon is not affordable. If your husband approves, by all means have professionals do the job they do so well. If you cannot afford salon care and you aren't talented in this area, look around you. There are friends with whom you can exchange favors. It will save money and cultivate friendships.

MAKEUP

One day I visited Wes's office in Baton Rouge. I felt something was not quite right as he greeted me and introduced me to a new colleague but had no idea what it was. I could tell Wes wasn't happy about something. In a stern manner he said to me later, "Bernie, I've never known you to go out without putting on makeup." Was I shocked! I was crushed. I had tried a new line and was pleased with the results. You can imagine my chagrin at his displeasure.

Don't make any big changes without passing it by your husband before introducing a new look publicly. Husbands are not always in on what fashion is up to, although we know there are exceptions. One husband may not notice his wife's short hairdo for two or three weeks. Another may notice if his wife moves the part in her hair. You must get to know the fellow you live with to understand how to fulfill his desires.

Your husband is interested in how you look, even though he may not show it in the complimentary way you'd prefer. Sometimes it takes an incident similar to mine to get a wife's attention, for her to know he cares about her appearance.

Our pastor in Baton Rouge was straight-laced, but he used to say, "Even an old barn looks better with a little coat of paint." The best quality makeup you can afford may have better staying power than a cheaper one, and you may receive better counsel from beauticians when you purchase it; however, you don't need to make a major investment to achieve the desired effect. The secret is to have healthy skin, which you may inherit or possess through general good health. Taking proper care of your skin does help.

Your "house" is going to wear out along with everyone else's who lives long enough. Allow yours to grow old gracefully. Remember, the lines on your face are character lines. The secret is to be beautiful inside, which should be our chief concern. Then use enhancements to make your facade better match the interior.

In brief, here is my advice for having an attractive face. Every day use a moisturizing sunscreen lotion under your makeup. Don't wait until you are concerned about sun damage. Drink plenty of water and make it a lifetime habit. Cleanliness and a little tender loving care are a must.

If you didn't inherit smooth, fine textured skin, you can't buy it in a bottle, but you can take care of what the Lord gave you. A dermatologist gave me sound advice which I have heeded for many years. I do not take long, soaking baths or lengthy showers. After bathing, I dry off with a damp washcloth rather than a towel. While my skin is still damp, I lather on a good moisturizing lotion. Water is the moisture needed by your skin, not oil.

You can make your skin look smoother and healthier with proper application of makeup. The art of makeup is a skill you can develop even if you aren't a natural at it. Take advantage of free aids—books, magazines, and consultants at makeup counters and salons. Put on your sales-resistance armor before seeking their advice, or you'll end up taking home items you will never use anyway.

Color analysis is neither a must nor an absolute science. If it were, all color analysts would agree. If it fits into your budget, I do think it will help to enhance your looks. Its greatest benefit for me has been in coordinating my wardrobe. Packing for trips is simplified because every item is interchangeable with others, and endless accessories are unnecessary. An added benefit is the confidence of wearing clothes in colors that compliment your complexion.

WALK

The way you move and hold your head and body can project energy. If you have become lazy about your walk, study yourself. The healthier you are, the more likely you are to walk with energy. Does your step tell others you feel good about yourself?

Please don't misinterpret what I say about outward appearance. We know God looks at the heart, but we can't ignore the fact that man looks on the outward. We are being unrealistic if we don't consider it important. A man forms his opinion and gets a message about who you are by what he sees, at least in the beginning.

I have observed people in bookstores picking up one volume instead of another simply because the cover looks more interesting. Why else do publishers design attractive dust jackets? Only an exceptional reader picks up a book with an unattractive cover. The same thing happens with people. You generally keep your first impression of someone tucked away in your mind for a long time, if not forever.

You needn't be the most beautiful for others to want to know you, but be the best you can by using all the uniqueness which God created in you. Attempt to make your cover match the book inside, sending the message "The Lord Jesus Christ Who loves you lives here."

We can't depend on our outward appearance for personal esteem, but we can look unto Jesus for our value as individuals. When we have done what we can, we won't allow others to reflect negative feelings back to us.

A peaceful, contented feeling comes over me when I think of my heavenly Father looking at me. He isn't comparing me to any of His other creations. He loves me as His very own special person. To Him I am beautiful. When I latch onto this thought, when I see myself through His eyes, I feel good about me. Doesn't it stimulate you to present your very best self to others both outwardly and inwardly?

With attention paid to all these aspects of personal care, you are ready to meet your husband's public and yours. You're ready to be "the expression of his glory;" to walk with the practiced grace that displays your inner attitude of confidence. You're a reflection of the kind of man you married (or the one he is becoming).

18
Protect Your Investment

If you are giving, giving, and giving, you are making an investment in something or someone. I challenge you to protect your investment. Since your husband is your number one earthly priority, I encourage you to take good care of that man—the most precious investment of your life.

DIET

One of the more difficult steps I took with my family was to change our eating habits years ago. Wes seemed skeptical of some of the ways I suggested. The children were dismayed at the prospect of life without white bread!

I had my own inner struggle with making the needed changes. During the early years of our marriage, I enjoyed Wes's nodding approval as I put tasty food on the table. I enjoyed the children's delight as sugary temptations were pulled from the oven. I wasn't sure I wanted to give up all that hearty approval and praise of my good cooking. During the gradual transition, I kept reminding myself, this too shall pass, counting on the idea that someday they will thank me.

Now the children are grown and gone. In their homes they have continued the healthful preparation and eating of good foods. This pleases me and I feel my decision of years ago is having an effect on my children's and grandchildren's health today.

Our goal of good health for our husbands must include close scrutiny of their diets, focusing on healthful foods and educating them as we go along. It takes time, effort, and creativity to bring about a change in people's eating habits. For some it's much more difficult than for others. We have been reared in a society that has taught us to eat what is attractive and tasty to us personally without much thought about its effect on our bodies. Fortunately, that is beginning to change.

Wes is given a complete physical examination each year by an internist. This type of specialist is very thorough and takes notice of every detail. On one of his visits, Wes pointed out an irritating, itchy rash. It was unattractive, especially during the summer when he was exposed to more sun. The affected areas would not tan, and his skin looked gray and ugly. The doctor told him he could go to a dermatologist and spend lots of money if he wanted to, but he would always have the rash. Even if it cleared up temporarily, it would return. Wes would just have to learn to live with it. I took that report as a challenge.

I began to read nutrition books for a clue and started a vitamin and mineral supplement program for him. Within a short time the rash was gone, never to appear again. That isn't to say you and I can replace doctors, but to point out that we have a responsibility for the health of our husbands. We are capable of tender loving care that no one else can give and need always to be studying and learning to improve the care we provide.

Wes had his third kidney stone in 1987. During his hospital stay, we learned he was having high blood pressure readings. At home, I took out the nutrition books and read more information about high blood pressure and diet. With weight control, a high fiber, low-fat diet, carefully selected supplements, and a consistent exercise program, his blood pressure was not only under control, but good. We were delighted that these efforts delayed the use of medication for five years.

I'm not saying we can always avoid health problems, but I am confirming what you already know. Extra love and care for your husband will pay big dividends. Many people inherit a body makeup that gives them the advantage of natural good health. How can we know what we inherited if we constantly bombard our "temples" with the wrong kind of food, especially if we also eat too much? He may never say so, but your husband will appreciate your concern for his health.

I believe we live until the Lord is ready for our departure from the earth. Good care of our bodies improves the quality of life but doesn't necessarily lengthen it. He "holds the keys" to death. He does not, however, promise us good health if we knowingly abuse our bodies. We must do our responsible part. It takes time, reading, learning, and openness to new ideas, but isn't all that part of making your husband and family a priority? I think so. Try to keep them on the best diet you can; they will love you for it **later**, if not now.

CLOTHES

In studying your own wardrobe, you'll probably come across information that will be useful to your husband. John Molloy warns men to follow his advice and not the advice of their wives. Rightly so, but you can change that idea. Read Mr. Molloy's book, along with other good ones about men's apparel and learn all you can about the clothing most appropriate for your husband, especially at work.

Know your man. Some don't appreciate their wives' messing around with their clothes or their closets. On the other hand, a fellow may love his wife to buy his clothes, and lay them out each day, matched and ready to go. You can help him in many ways if he is willing. Consider his build and his coloring. You probably know his budget and can learn what's right for his job. The more knowledgeable you are, the better your advice.

Because of Wes's particular situation, he strongly approves of Mr. Molloy's book, *Dress for Success*. His company generally gives it to all new hires. Mr. Molloy's recommendations are not necessarily based on what looks best on the individual but how the public responds to people dressed in different styles and colors. I read the book very carefully and marked all that was pertinent to Wes's choice of clothes. I made a small chart to fit into his billfold showing his particular requirements, so he doesn't have to depend upon memory on the rare occasions when he shops.

For twenty-nine years I ironed Wes's shirts—white, long-sleeved dress shirts. I felt very possessive of this chore and I hated to give it up. It was something I could do for him personally. I began doing it when we purchased our first washing machine, and we calculated how many years of ironing his shirts would pay for it. Ultimately, it became one of the loving touches I was proud of.

"You must give up something, or you'll kill yourself," Wes said as our lives expanded to include so much. He had to take the job away from me.

Do you have one or two things you do for your husband that go the extra mile of concern and affection? Ironing those shirts was only one way I found to demonstrate my concern for Wes's welfare on a daily basis. You can look for others; you know what would speak to your husband individually. It may be shining his shoes occasionally, pairing up his socks more carefully, cooking the venison stored way back in the freezer, or straightening out his fishing tackle. I don't know, but I bet you do.

In choosing your husband's clothes you should consider appropriateness and the best quality your budget can afford. He may be color blind and need your help. If he is, encourage him to buy items such as socks all in one color. Suggest that he stay in the same color family for all his apparel so he'll always look well put together. A good clothier is a great help, and making friends of a special clerk is excellent strategy. Shopping together is a time for you to learn about his likes and dislikes. You will also have a store of useful information when it's time to purchase a gift.

Ideally, if it pleases your man, shop together for his clothes. It's a wonderful opportunity to build his morale. You can use shopping trips to polish his armor a little bit, not with flattery but with sincere compliments that make him feel good about himself.

WEIGHT

Be careful of your man's ego and morale if this is a sensitive area for him. Overemphasis can bring the opposite of what you desire. You can help most by slowly adding the proper items to his diet. The earlier you develop a taste for the correct foods, the more likely you are to be eating them for a lifetime.

Your greatest contribution is in well-prepared and carefully planned meals at home that are heavy on vegetables and other high-fiber foods and light on red meats, fats, sodium, and refined sugar. You need to rethink the food groups and consult the newest information on the food pyramid.

Try to approach his weight problem through proper nutrition, encouraging exercise, and giving positive reinforcement. Your focus is good health not looks, although that is usually a fringe benefit. Whenever appropriate, praise his obvious or not so obvious efforts to conquer it. Be sure he knows your motive is love for him.

EXERCISE

Some men are sports freaks but limit their participation to a weekend of sitting in front of the television or as stadium spectators. In all the imaginative ways you can dream up, encourage him to be active in some kind of exercise. You need a walking buddy, so that's a good choice.

When there is a special occasion and the budget allows, buy a gift like an exercise bike, a pedometer, or jogging clothes to encourage him. Keep your man's temperament in mind and be sharp to spot items which might entice him into physical activity.

WEALTH

Many couples have the majority of their arguments and cold or hot wars over spending or saving family income. Communicating will be the greatest help. By taking time together to outline your budget and goals, you can avoid a lot of disagreements. To be in accord about debt and an overall philosophy of handling money makes for peace on the homefront. "Keep out of debt and owe no man anything, except to love one another" (Romans 13:8a). If possible, there should be a mutual concept, "our" money. "Mine" and "yours" are divisive terms that may cause potential problems.

When Wes and I were first married, one of his early decisions was to hand the checkbook to me and say, "You've had a lot of bookkeeping, so you're better at this than I am." Innocently, I jumped right in to do the very best I could. Thirty years later, I laid the job down when he said he would take over. I love it. I may be better at it, but I doubt it and frankly, I don't care. I still reconcile the bank statements, and that makes it a team effort. He does a great job of paying the bills and keeping our papers in order. Even if he didn't, I'd love his doing it, and let me tell you why. Having the wife write the checks and reconcile the bank statement is not a bad arrangement, but it may not be as wise as some think. You may be very good at bookkeeping or have a better head for figures and spending than he does. There is, however, something about a husband's innocent questions, "Honey, how much money do we have left? What happened to all the money?" It can be interpreted as asking, "What did **you** do with all the money?"

Finances should be an area for caution. Women have a tendency to take on responsibility for the money rather than just the book-keeping. They feel frustration and anxiety when there are more bills than money at the end of the month. I found it difficult to do the job without assuming the responsibility. Wes's trust made my job easier, but it was still an emotional struggle. A lot depends on your personality and whether you have a tendency to overspend. Before entering such an arrangement, be sure you are on the same wave length and have a similar outlook about finances.

I know there is no ideal way for all couples. I think the best arrangement is for both to participate to some degree. There are many aspects to be considered: time, temperament, talent, and **harmony**. When the wife takes part in handling family finances, she is more likely to be considerate and concerned about proper money management.

"The heart of her husband trusts in her confidently *and* relies on and believes in her securely" (Proverbs 31:11a). Your husband should be able to trust you completely about money. If not, you **must** earn a new reputation with him. Too often I've heard a wife make comments such as "I've had this for quite awhile," when truthfully she had bought the dress and hidden it away for a few days in her closet. "What he doesn't know won't hurt him." In reality it will hurt, not only him but most of all you and the trust between the two of you should he ever learn of your attitude. I believe he'll recognize your deceit, and distrust will spread to other areas.

Are you someone who bums money off friends, gets one to charge something on her credit card, or makes special arrangements with shops to hide purchases from your husband? Label it what you will, dear lady, you are being deceptive and no amount of excuses can justify such behavior.

Improper spending or even saying "I want" too often may make your husband feel disquieted because it shows a lack of confidence in his money-making capabilities. Surely it's not your intention to make him feel inadequate. You have chosen to be the kind of wife God wants you to be. If you feel you cannot get a grip on your wanter, seek help from a Christian financial counselor. Learn good financial principles through reading the excellent books on the subject that are available in libraries and bookstores.

While growing up, Wes and I were blessed to learn solid financial principles from our parents' example. They very seldom explained the reasons for their method of managing money or the lack of it, but we picked up a few guidelines along the way: Never spend more than you have, and never spend as much as you have. If young couples follow these two simple rules, they won't have the enormous financial burdens we see in so many families.

When our first child was born my parents gave us some money, a small amount by today's standard. "Start a savings account for Jamey," they said, and we did. Through their encouragement and contributions to the cause, we established a small fund for each of our children at birth. We added to each one every year as the Lord provided. ". . . For children are not duty bound to lay up store for their parents, but parents for their children" (II Corinthians 12:14).

Near college time, each child was given the management of the fund to be used according to a specific plan. Their dad scrutinized the plan and gave his approval if it was sound. That included purchasing cars, but they became totally responsible for insurance and up-keep. All the children supplemented the funds through summer or after school jobs. They had a lot of freedom with managing the money as long as they realized it must cover all of their college expenses. We were pleased to see the experience play an important role in their learning solid financial principles.

I hope you are being a "her husband trusts in her" wife not one who fears he will find her careless with money. That includes having a weakness for shopping malls and boutiques. Is it time for you to confess a spending problem, ask forgiveness, and form new habits of responsibility?

KEEP HUMOR IN HIS LIFE

Give him toys that will make him laugh and involve him in fun. Wes has accumulated some neat ones that he and the grandchildren all enjoy. Our first Christmas alone I gave Wes an electric train, a replica of a Colorado mining train. He has made it a tradition for the base of the Christmas tree and enjoys sharing it with each child. I gave him a motorized submarine he enjoys running in our pool. Even some of his business associates love a turn at the controls. The children's favorite stories are about his exploits with a radio-controlled model airplane. Each year when colleagues inquire about what to buy him at Christmas, I suggest they include some kind of toy.

Save up funny stories to share at mealtimes, especially ones about yourself. When you hear a good joke, store it away. He will probably steal some of your jokes and stories to tell at the office. When you contribute light, amusing conversation, it helps him to laugh at his day. It encourages him to let go of burdens that can be taken up the next day and enjoy the moment.

PUT A TIGER IN HIS TANK

You can strike chords within your husband's heart as no one else! You know his soft, emotional, vulnerable spots and his off-limits territory. Cherish that position and guard it safely. Don't talk too freely with others about the intimate side of your marriage.

In the sexual relationship, the difference between men and women again becomes evident. A wife is always affected by the atmosphere of her day and their *whole* life together. A husband is more likely to be affected by his *immediate* need and the *mood* of the moment. You may be thinking that he forgot your birthday last week, and he's thinking about how good you look right now.

When you were dating, you held hands and thought how romantic, how soft and tender your relationship was. He was thinking, Wow, if her hand feels this good, I bet her shoulder feels terrific. We are *different*, aren't we? Guess who will do most of the adjusting? You remember, I am sure—"adapted, completing, suitable." As a woman, you will understand the differences more readily than he.

Most men think that if they walk across the bedroom in the nude, their wives will love it and be turned on. Books and counselors say that women are not as stimulated through the eye gate as men are, but you'll never convince him! A man is similar to a peacock and enjoys doing a little strutting. I'm sure he likes to strut for an appreciative audience.

Are you going to be miserable sitting here waiting for him to be like you, or are you going to get with the program? Make a choice. Accept the fact that you can't make your husband *feel* as you do. Choose to live in the moment. You can bring your emotions under the rule of your spirit by an act of your will. The more often you make your emotions submit to your spirit, the more frequently and quickly you will be able to do it, but I'm not sure it ever becomes easier. It's a new decision every time. The bottom line is **you** make the choice. Knowing that your husband doesn't assess your day when he puts his arms around you in the evening might help you understand how he has forgotten the angry words at breakfast. To have a wonderful sex life with your husband, the greatest contribution you can make is *unselfishness.*

You have the privilege of making a Spirit-controlled decision every time you go into the bedroom with your husband. It will always benefit both of you. You can make or break your husband's morale more quickly and completely in the bedroom than anywhere else. Choose to give rather than being concerned about your needs. The most wonderful benefit comes to a woman when she gives unselfishly. Her needs will be met in ways she had never dreamed.

Tremendous harm can be done through something the world encourages—fantasizing. Don't follow that advice. Satan uses fantasizing to get you into untold trouble. Keep alert; the mind has plenty of temptations with intruding thoughts from the enemy. Whether you fantasize about a real or an imaginary person, your husband can never live up to what you can conjure up in your mind. Fantasy will make you more vulnerable to other men and gullible about their flattery. Beware!

Never, never use sex as reward or punishment. Many wives still do so after years of marriage. Sex is a means of communicating love, forgiveness, pleasure, delight in one another, and total unselfishness. If you spend this precious time with your husband going over unpleasant memories, you will never experience the peace of giving. I doubt you will provide anything more than temporary physical pleasure.

The news media, magazines, movies, and our educational system are full of misinformation about sex. Sexual stimuli abound in everyday life, and bad philosophy and pornography of all kinds is easily available. Do what you can to encourage your husband to protect himself and your sons from exposure. Don't let down your guard against inappropriate sexual behavior. A sweet, loving, submissive attitude and honest, straight-forward communication are your best defenses.

With his sexual needs met by his wife, a husband is better armed to face the day, any trial, and any home-threatening woman on the prowl. He will feel good in at least one area—the love of his wife.

IDENTITY

Most every man I know who does well attaches his identify to his job. When retirement comes, a man may have difficulty thinking redirection rather than "it is all over." If your husband were to lose his job, he might face the same kind of struggle. You can't do it for him, but you can help him to recognize that he's important outside of his work in all the ways I have mentioned.

BUT WHY?

"I'm doing all this," you may say as you read this chapter. Yet underneath perhaps you've been waiting for the return on your investment. When you realize there has been none and you are disappointed, it would be good to look again at your priorities and goals. Have no hidden agenda except the heart peace and joy which come from being all God wants **you** to be.

Only you and the Lord know why you do what you do. He always looks at our hearts and knows our motives. Years ago Wes and I listened to a tape about motives, and the central message has stayed with us both as a helpful principle in our lives.

Everything you do comes from one of three motives: fear—of what you might lose; hope—of what you might gain; or love—of what you might give. If you serve and love your husband in the *fear* of what you might lose, you have already lost. If you serve and love your husband in the *hope* of what you might gain, you get only temporary satisfaction. If you serve and love your husband in the *love* of what you might give, you are gaining temporary satisfaction and the eternal reward of "Well done, you upright (honorable, admirable) and faithful servant!" (Matthew 25:21a).

19

In The Gates

The people who work with or for your husband should hold you in high regard. Their opinion will be based on many things such as your looks, clothes, and conversation, but the strongest impression you can make will be with your attitude. Basic rules of common courtesy and kindness are of utmost importance. If he has a secretary, be especially sure to treat her with respect and consideration. She plays an important role in the lives of both of you. If she is your friendly acquaintance, you can work together to keep schedules in order and agree on protecting your husband's time.

You should never treat his secretary or anyone under his authority in a subservient manner. Always ask his permission before you make any special request of anyone in his office. As time passes, you'll understand what he expects and what will bring disapproval.

Your husband should never have to be concerned about your being congenial with his secretary, other business associates, or their wives. Some people are not as likable as others, but part of your role is to overlook flaws and "instead, in the true spirit of humility (lowliness of mind) let each regard the others as better than and superior to himself [thinking more highly of one another than you do of yourselves]" (Philippians 2:3).

Be cautious about discussing business matters with anyone. Your husband may tell you something he never intends others to know. He undoubtedly prefers no one to know that he discusses such matters with you.

Never show disapproval of your husband in front of his associates. Your moments of airing a grievance with him should be private. An ant hill can quickly become Mount Everest if it is exposed in front of others.

Call your husband at work only for something important. Men get an undesirable reputation when too much of their workday is taken up with personal calls or when their wives frequently want them to run errands. It shouldn't appear to others that their wives are leading and directing their households.

Always conduct yourself in a ladylike manner that is above reproach. Other men will envy your husband. Sometimes a man will think a woman is flirting with him when he has no reason to. We must guard our behavior so no one will ever have a basis for that assumption.

There may be occasions when you'll be the recipient of critical comments, rejection, and even open hostility. You must be armed with an answer, wise in your timing, and cautious with your words.

"Let your speech at all times be gracious (pleasant and winsome), seasoned [as it were] with salt, [so that you may never be at a loss] to know how you ought to answer anyone [who puts a question to you]" (Colossians 9:6). Look for opportunities to share your testimony with others, but stay within your husband's guidelines, particularly when you are on his business turf. Encourage him to witness as often as opportunities come.

I remember one encounter vividly: we were flying to a meeting on a small airplane. Several couples were aboard, but the men and women were seated separately. As we three wives relaxed and chatted on the flight, the other Christian wife and I discussed some recent exciting experiences. Wes's boss's wife grew agitated. When my friend began her personal testimony, the lady exploded. She spoke harshly to my friend but directed most of her accusations at me. As we left the plane, I was deeply concerned. I wasn't disturbed that we had used this opportunity to share Christ, but I was apprehensive about telling Wes what had happened. He didn't react disapprovingly, but I saw his brow furrow.

Though there was tension between the lady and me as the meeting went on, I tried hard to behave in a normal manner. We had no contact in the weeks that followed until the time came for a special couples trip to California. Since she had made no attempt to contact me, I went with a degree of anxiety. I made a definite commitment to forgiveness and loving behavior. I asked the Lord to inspire in me a way to reach out to her, and He did! I bought a book I knew she would be especially glad to receive. When I dropped by her room with it, she invited me in. As we began a rather awkward conversation, she seemed to relax and talked about different subjects it appeared she had saved for just such a time. We had a lovely visit, and there was no weight that could hold me on the floor as I left her room. The comment she made will live a long time in my memory.

"Do you remember . . . ? I've been wanting to write to you or something but decided to wait for a chance to tell you in person. What I should have told you that day was what a wonderful person you really are."

I'm not going to tell you that if you always obey the Lord, are nice and forgiving, all will turn out fine. That was one of the times it went well for me, and I praise the Lord that it did.

Instead of dreading company get-togethers because of the great differences in people, accept these events as exciting challenges. It is a wonderful time to be what you are—"You are the salt of the earth . . . the light of the world. A city set on a hill cannot be hidden" (Matthew 5:13,14). And who knows, there may be more opportunities to tell others that Christ is the difference.

One evening on a company trip a young wife wept as she disclosed her problems. I told her about Christ in my life and how He enabled me to go on in spite of tough circumstances.

"I always knew there was something different about you," she said. "I was sure you had to face many of the same situations I do, but now I see Jesus is the difference."

As a born-again woman out in the marketplace, you'll find your integrity under constant scrutiny. People look for an excuse to reject God's people, so guard your speech, behavior, and attitudes to avoid giving any. The same applies wherever you go, but in your husband's business place, you need to be especially sensitive. After all, you are part of him and want to be a picture that pleases him.

20

Is The Castle Suited to the King?

$\mathcal{D}$oes your husband think of his house as "home, sweet home," the way he wants it to be? Or is it the showcase you want it to be? Is it messed up enough to be comfortable but cleaned up enough to be orderly? If the atmosphere is one in which he feels comfortable and the daily schedule revolves around his, your king will surely enjoy coming home to his castle.

When our children were small, people counseled us not to have dinner late because the children needed to be in bed early. I never fed them before their dad arrived. They were allowed a hearty snack in the afternoon after school that helped them wait more patiently for a late dinner. Wes always worked long hours, so the children did their homework, took baths, and were dressed for bed by the time he got home. Then we sat down to eat together. I thought those family meals were important for all of us, no matter how late we had to eat. I have never regretted the decision. You must choose what is best for your own family.

Sometimes I had a terrible attitude about Wes's lateness, and remembering that is painful. When a wife has a wrong attitude, everyone in the family catches it. When I had a bad attitude, we were often irritated with him before he came in the door. Then I joyfully think of when I began to change my attitude. What an impact it had on our family.

Some difficulties must be attacked head on with humor. We were having lasagna, one of our favorites. Wes was very late and the aroma was causing a frenzy of impatience. We carefully removed the lasagna from the big casserole, leaving a small square in the middle. When he arrived home, we told him we couldn't wait any longer, but had put some left-overs in the oven for him.

"What fun we had preparing to tease Dad," says Juli, though none of us believe we fooled him for a minute.

The one piece of furniture our son wanted from our home was the round oak dining table. He collected many fond memories around that table. Had I done the approved thing and fed my children early and put them to bed, they would have missed those treasured times of family sharing.

If you could check it out with our grown children, they would tell you that meals were one of the greatest times at our house. They always welcomed their dad with love and excitement. I have a vivid memory of seeing Wes walk in and cross the kitchen with four small bodies clinging to his legs and riding his feet. He missed a transition from work to home, but the obvious joy of his arrival more than compensated for it.

In meeting your husband at his castle door, be warm, loving, and filled with excited anticipation. Knowing him well will enable you to greet him in the way he most appreciates. Many men are ready for quiet. They want to be welcomed calmly and left alone for a while. You'll have to determine what works best.

Even if your husband is away from home a lot on business, your attitude still plays a major role. The attitude of the whole family should be "we will do things things to please our dad as though he were here right now and knew exactly what was happening." Such thinking deters anyone's feeling that dad is an intruder when he gets back.

I've found that men like orderliness except for the messiness they create. If your husband is more comfortable with a little clutter around, you must determine what both of you can live with. But never ignore his preference, even though it may be the opposite of your own.

Your husband will value your role in the home if you have a healthy regard for what you do. Never be guilty of apologetically saying, "I am *just* a housewife." It's better to consider yourself a homemaker *first*, even if you have an outside career or ministry. Show pride and respect for what you are, what both you and your husband have chosen; it frees you to enjoy all that you do each day. You'll see the job as a part of the big picture, building lives and not just maintaining a house.

If he is like most men, there are certain elements your husband would want in his home.

Relaxation. He can relax in the atmosphere he enjoys most. Study his favorite spot carefully and see if there is a *feel* about it you can project into other parts of the house.

Comfort. He must feel *at ease* when at home and not like an intruder. The furniture should suit him and it would be nice if there were places where he feels especially comfortable.

Orderliness. Men seem to like you to know **exactly** where things are when they need them. We can always go back to the good old advice, "a place for everything and everything in its place." I want my house in order, but it is a constant effort for me. It's worth the trouble as you reap the benefits of saving time, not losing articles, and feeling good about your surroundings.

Peace. If he is a man who loves unrest and war, you can teach him the value of peace by being a peacemaker, a pleasant person, and providing an atmosphere of serenity.

A man may be a time waster himself, but he respects those who aren't. Homemakers are notorious for being time wasters. If you are one of them, you can begin to make changes. Be honest with yourself, and remember you aren't wasting time, you're wasting **life**. Control the use of your time or it will control you. It ticks on regardless of what you do with it. The atmosphere of your home will often be determined by how you manage your day.

Read, listen, and observe how others arrange their schedules. Follow sound advice about housecleaning methods, paperwork, telephone time, and visiting with friends. Keep your list of priorities in sight and in your heart. Make what you do reflect them, and you will be happy with the results.

A man who is successful or is about to be, needs a haven at the end of his day. Do everything you can to make his home your man's refuge from the battlefield of work and the troubles of the world. When men talk about memories, their comments reveal much about their mothers, families, and homes. You are building memories for your children and your husband—reinforcing those of the home he came from or providing healing from his early life.

Home can give your husband courage to meet the next day's problems. Home must be someone's priority, or it will be nothing but an empty shell, a place of existence. The Scriptures tell us that we girls should learn "to be self-controlled, chaste, homemakers, good natured (kind hearted). . ." (Titus 3:5). Suit your castle to your king, and learn to be the homemaker you should be. The price is costly for a house where "home, sweet home" is not grown!

Many daughters have done virtuously, nobly and well [with the strength of character that is steadfast in goodness], but you excel them all. Charm and grace are deceptive, and beauty is vain [because it is not lasting], but a woman who reverently and worshipfully fears the Lord, she shall be praised! Give her of the fruit of her hands, and let her own works praise her in the gates of the city!

—Proverbs 31:29-31

21
You Excel Them All

$\mathcal{V}$ery early in the morning I moved quietly around our bedroom trying to get dressed without awakening Wes. I felt pretty good about my efforts as his heavy breathing continued and smugly thought he was getting the well-deserved rest he needed.

I left the dressing room and tiptoed across the floor.

"Bernie, you're a good woman!" I heard Wes say from the bed. We'd been married a long time, and he wasn't verbally expressive or free with compliments. I could never remember his making such a comment before. Joy welled up in my heart. He has said it many times since, I am glad to say, but that first time was so very special. It seemed one of the times the Lord reached out and made a sunflower pop up out of the pavement of my life to say "I love you." At that moment I felt I had been given a giant bear hug. Echoing in my memory came the words, "and her husband boasts of *and* praises

189

her, [saying], Many daughters have done virtuously, nobly, *and* well [with the strength of character that is steadfast in goodness], but you excel them all" (Proverbs 31:28b,29).

My aim has been to impress upon you that your motive must be to please God, to be who and what He created you to be. Your reward (my 100 percent money-back guarantee) is not that your husband will change or that your efforts will produce results in his life. It is that if you begin to do the things I have shared, you will have a peace and joy beyond all understanding.

I pray you have made commitments as you read these pages. The thoughts I have written about come from my own life through many mistakes and abuses of God's principles. Where I seem to have boasted, I must say, I boast only in the Lord Jesus Christ. Every example would have been one of failure if not for the things He has done.

I have renewed my commitments as I shared with you and am excited to see what God has in store for me. My temple may be growing older, but my heart is as young as ever, and I can and will continue to grow. Good, bad, or indifferent, I rejoice to know I can receive all that comes from His hand.

Whatever happens with your husband, I pray you will do those things that please the Lord and He will reward you with serenity, present-day satisfaction, and eternal joy. Who knows, along the way maybe you, too, will hear those sweet words and know the depth of their meaning—"Honey, you're a good woman!"

Information

For information on Mrs. Cantrell's speaking availability, please contact her at the following address:

4041 Randall Mill Road NW
Atlanta, GA 30327
Phone: 404/231-0717
Fax: 770/621-1011

To order additional copies of this book, send $14.95 per copy plus $2 shipping and handling to:

Sower's Press
P.O. Box 666306
Marietta, GA 30066
Phone/Fax: 770/977-3784
Toll-Free: 1-888-977-1079

A companion Study Guide is available for $6.95. Contact the above address for information on quantity discounts.